THE
LOGAN STORY

What God hath wrought through the lives of
WALLACE AND RUTH LOGAN

THE SEQUEL TO A MAN CALLED SAKUUNDA

THE
LOGAN STORY
What God hath wrought through the lives of
WALLACE AND RUTH LOGAN

COMPILED BY
DAVID LOGAN AND FAMILY

Part 1 of this book
A MAN CALLED SAKUUNDA
Previously published by
Voices from the Vineyard
Missionary Corp.

THE LOGAN STORY
By: David Logan and Family
Copyright © 2010
GOSPEL FOLIO PRESS
All Rights Reserved

Published by
GOSPEL FOLIO PRESS
304 Killaly St. W.
Port Colborne, ON L3K 6A6
CANADA

ISBN: 9781897117989

Cover design by Rachel Brooks

All Scripture quotations from the
King James Version unless otherwise noted.

Printed in USA

Contents

Acknowledgements 7
Introduction.. 9

PART 1
A MAN CALLED SAKUUNDA BY PAUL LOGAN

Introduction to A Man Called Sakuunda............................ 13
Desperate Situation 15
Something Better.. 17
Romance.. 19
Skulls and Idols... 21
Proving God 23
Fiery Trials... 25
White Man, Can You Help Me?... 27
Deadly Poison 29
Committed 31
Treasures From Darkness.. 33
A Hundredfold 35
I Am Ready 37
Father... 40
A Challenge 40
The Gap 41

PART 2
STORIES AND LETTERS

Early Life.. 45
Early African Life.. 49
Heathenism 59
Vision to Reach People with the Gospel............................ 69
Medical.. 95

Missionary Life 99
Humour... 101
Obedience to the Word: Spiritual Growth....................... 105
God's Protection 109
Everyday Events at Chavuma 121
God's Provision... 123
Salvation.. 133
Christian Challenge.. 143
Faith Tested.. 151
Prayer 157
Tabernacle News.. 165
Letters of General Interest... 169
Chavuma 1923-1967 175
Looking Back... 183
Looking Ahead.. 189

Acknowledgements

Without God's love for mankind and the work of our Mediator and Redeemer, the Lord Jesus Christ, this story could never have been written.

But God DID *"so love the world that He gave His only begotten Son, that whosoever believeth on Him should not perish, but have everlasting life!"*

So we thank God for the message of salvation that took Wallace and Ruth Logan to Africa to share this Good News.

We thank the Lord for the example of their lives to each of us in the family.

Specifically, regarding the book, we express our appreciation to Mr. Sam Robinson, President Emeritus of Christian Missions in Many Lands who gave us much encouragement to pursue this endeavor, and has exhibited much patience in waiting for the final result.

Special thanks is given to our cousin, Mrs. Martha Sacher Wilson who gave us a treasury of personal letters written by Father and Mother to her parents, Fred and Louise Sacher, which have been saved over many, many years. This made it possible to include more examples of God's power and faithfulness as well as to verify details important to the accounts.

Also, we thank all who have contributed to the writing of this book by way of their faithful prayers, sharing of African pictures, offering ideas and providing encouragement.

Voices from the Vinyard Missionary Corporation, now known as Christian Missions in Many Lands, has granted permission to reprint *A Man Called Sakuunda* as the first part of this book, for which we are very grateful. Additionally, CMML has also granted us permission to reprint "The Fuel Pump" from the May 2004 issue of Missions magazine as well as the article "What God Hath Wrought" which appeared in the Fall 1967 issue. Thank you.

To Mr. Sam Cairns and Gospel Folio Press for editing this manuscript, preparing the manuscript for publication and putting all the finishing touches in the perfect place we extend our grateful thanks.

To Mrs. Marilyn (Woodward) MacMullen we express our appreciation for working on the manuscript with the expertise of an English major and the background experience of living in Zambia for a time.

It is our desire and prayer that this book exalt and honor the Lord Jesus Christ.

May it be so!

Ben and Frances (Logan) Iler
Mike and Esther (Logan) Howell
John and Eleanor (Logan) Sims
Bob and Viola (Logan) Young
David and Grace (Logan) Croudace
Paul and Lois Logan
David and Ruth Ann Logan

Introduction

Many of the Lord's people who heard Wallace Logan tell of the power of God to save, sustain and safeguard in Central Africa, have asked that a sequel be written to the book, *A Man Called Sakuunda* which would document further occurrences of a mighty God working through ordinary people to bring praise to His great name.

Wallace and Ruth's children and their spouses have responded to these requests and have written in this book about other occurrences in their lives.

This is not an account of a great and remarkable couple, but rather the affirmation of the magnitude of the love, grace and power of a great and mighty God who accomplishes His will through commonplace people who are yielded to Him.

You will find the book in two sections. Part 1, entitled *A Man Called Sakuunda*, was written by Paul Logan shortly after his father's home call and was presented by Voices from the Vineyard Missionary Corporation (now CMML) to those who attended the World Missions Congress in 1969.

Part 2 is a collection of many of the stories from Central Africa that captured the attention of hundreds of audiences. Segments of many letters written by Wallace and Ruth are also included so that incidents can be told "in their own words."

May God be glorified! And may you be encouraged in your most holy faith!

"Oh, the depth of the riches both of the wisdom and knowledge of God! How unsearchable are His judgments and His ways past finding out! For who has known the mind of the LORD? Or who has become His counselor? Or who has first given to Him and it shall be repaid to him? For of Him and through Him and to Him are all things, to Whom be glory forever. Amen" (Rom. 11:33-36).

Part 1
A Man Called
SAKUUNDA

By Paul Logan

Appreciation is expressed to all the family
for their help in compiling this book.
—PAUL LOGAN

Introduction to
A Man Called Sakuunda

These brief sketches from the life of Wallace Falconer Logan were assembled in book form as a challenge for each one attending World Missions Congress 1969. Early this year, after serving our Lord Jesus Christ 46 years in the heart of Africa, our highly esteemed and beloved brother was called into his Saviour's presence.

Voices from the Vineyard Missionary Corp. takes pleasure in presenting you this gift with the prayer that God will use it in your life for His honor and glory.

"I beseech you therefore, brethren, by the mercies of God, that ye present your bodies a living sacrifice, holy, acceptable unto God, which is your reasonable service. And be not conformed to this world: but be ye transformed by the renewing of your mind, that ye may prove what is that good, and acceptable, and perfect, will of God" (Rom. 12:1-2).

Desperate Situation

Cycling along the narrow, winding foot-path in Central Africa, Wallace Logan's thoughts were miles away. The path straightened and he increased his speed. Suddenly—just ahead, he saw a huge snake! It was lying right across the bush track. He was going too fast to stop! There was only one thing to do— that was to run over it. Bump, bump went the two tires. He became so excited that he fell off. Furious, the snake darted toward its fallen victim and reared up to strike. Wallace was caught in a half sitting position. In desperation he glanced around for a suitable weapon. All he could see nearby was a rotten chunk of wood.

He grabbed it, threw it—but missed! The enraged serpent turned and struck for the wood, crushing it in its jaws. Then like lightning, it turned and was ready to strike at him! Any moment now, he would be in a death of agony! What a predicament! Lying helpless before this infuriated enemy! Hadn't God promised to be his strong tower when he left the States? Yet here he was, facing death in his early twenties. What was he doing here? Why was he here? Who was this man?

...And so here was Wallace in Central Africa taking the gospel to a heathen village, but now lying helpless before a deadly snake ready to strike. It was only a few feet away! A sudden move would cause the serpent to strike immediately! As he waited in fascinated horror, the seconds seemed like minutes, and the minutes like hours. Yet, the snake did not strike!

Wallace looked closer. The snake's mouth was open—and then he saw the reason. When the snake had bitten into the wood, a piece had jammed between its jaws, preventing it from closing its mouth. Quickly he found a stronger weapon and destroyed the snake. God had used the rotten wood which had missed its target, to save the life of His servant. When telling the story, Wallace would say, "*'The Name of the Lord is a strong tower; the righteous runneth into it, and is safe.'* That day I fell into it, but was safe just the same."

Something Better

Wallace Falconer Logan was born in Buffalo, New York, December 10, 1896. Although the family were church members, they did not know what it was to be born again. It all started with the witness of a German Christian who did not let his broken English hinder him from witnessing to Wallace and his gang. As a result, at the age of nineteen, he realized he needed to be saved from sin by receiving Jesus Christ as his own personal Saviour. He prayed asking God to save him.

It wasn't long before the devil tried to bring doubts to his mind concerning past sins. The Lord spoke to him through His Word: *"Thy sins and thy iniquities will I remember no more."*

"Thank you Lord," he exclaimed. "If you don't remember them, then why should I?" From that day on, he never doubted his salvation again.

Now a Christian, he realized that Christ was not only his Saviour but also his Lord. There was not going to be any half-hearted Christian service for the One who loved and gave Himself for him. It was going to be whole-hearted and complete surrender. He owed his life, his strength, his talents, his money, his all and all to God. He would frequently say, "What is the use in living, unless you can spend your life for the Man of Calvary."

Right from the start he had a burning passion to see souls saved. This vision did not dim even in the sunset of his life.

"My first missionary work," he would say, "was to win my own family to Christ." He entered his home and told them the news of his salvation. Their reaction shook him. His mother said, "You're crazy!" His father turned on him with, "Get away from here with your nonsense."

Although stunned by this reception, he was not discouraged. A new-found joy in Jesus Christ cannot be dampened that easily! He kept on witnessing.

He told the gang what had happened in his life. "Logan, we'll give you two weeks," they said, certain this would be plenty of time for the 'religious fanatic' to forget his foolishness.

Would he be able to stand? Would the attacks of Satan be too much for him? How much did the One on Whom he had so recently believed mean to him?

His old friends tried all sorts of means to persuade him to resume the old ways. Wallace prayed for wisdom in answering their entreaties to return to the old life. While studying the book of Hebrews one day, he was impressed by the number of times the word 'better' was used. What a Christian has in Christ is far better than what the world has to offer. Here was his answer. Next time he was offered a drink he replied, "No thank you, I have something better."

"Logan, come, let's go to the dance."

"No thank you, I have something better," would be his reply.

Curiosity overcame them, and before long he was asked, "What is it you have that's better?"

"I have Christ."

"So you're one of those religious fanatics?" they asked.

"No, I have something better than religion."

Although bewildered at first, they listened as he explained the thrill of living a life yielded to Christ. He was absolutely convinced that in Christ he had something lasting, and far better than the world could offer. Their interest was aroused, and so there was many an opportunity to talk about Christ, which led to some of the gang also finding 'something better.'

His mother one day told him, "Wallace, I don't want any more of your gospel tracts. I know more about religion than you do. I've read the Bible seven times!" However, he did not stop giving her tracts, and God used one of these to bring her to Christ. Eventually he had the joy of seeing his whole family come to the Saviour.

Some time later, his mother confessed, "Wallace, I don't know what book it was that I read seven times, but it certainly wasn't the Bible, because I am reading it now and it is a completely different book."

Romance

Old school friends were contacted in an effort to lead them to the Lord. Wallace was on fire for God. He witnessed to many in his home town of Buffalo, New York. Scores of people were converted as a result of the Walden Avenue Mission, and Bible studies in homes which he conducted. He was working together with an enthusiastic team of Christian young people including a keen Christian girl, Ruth Sacher. One task undertaken, was that of placing a tract in every home in the city of Buffalo. God blessed this effort.

Pretty, dark-haired Ruth was a dynamo of energy and full of zeal for the Lord. She was the youngest daughter of a family of ten which had come to Christ through reading a Bible given to the family. Although prepared to go through life single, while doing visitation work, Wallace began to realize the limitations of a single man in the Lord's service. He invited Ruth to go with him on visitation. When friends kidded her about this fine young man, she was quick to say, "There's nothing to it. It's strictly business in the Lord's work!" An amused, understanding smile was the usual response.

The Sachers loved young people and their home was always open to them. Wallace enjoyed this opportunity of getting acquainted with Christian young people, and with one in particular!

God burdened him for the lost in foreign lands. Exercised at first about serving the Lord in India, when hearing Gavin Mowat present the need in Central Africa, the Lord challenged him, "Who will go?"

He answered, "Here am I, Lord, send me."

Not knowing how Ruth felt about going to the foreign mission field, he was willing to give up prospects of marriage to serve the Lord there. He asked the Lord for a sign to indicate if Ruth was also burdened for Africa. When visiting the hospitals and jails one day with God's Word, he and Ruth paused on the street as crowds of people were thronging out of the armory. Ruth commented, "Doesn't that remind you of the teeming millions without Christ in Africa!"

This was just what he had been waiting for! Here was the Lord's go-ahead! The way was now clear to express his deepening feelings for the girl he had grown to love very dearly. He proposed to Ruth, but gave her a week to think it over and pray about it. When she said yes, he was so overjoyed, he formally shook her hand!

Wallace and Ruth presented their burden for those dying without Christ in Africa to their home assembly in Buffalo, for their fellowship and prayer. Then came a time of testing, one which faces many young people considering the mission field — the period of awaiting commendation by the local church. This experience was to be a valuable lesson in patience in God's school, fitting them to face frustrating trials later on. They were able to say, "Lord, if it is not your will for us to go, we are willing to remain; but if it is your will for us to go, then no man will be able to hinder us!"

So they waited. God answered prayer and they were commended to the work in Central Africa.

In March 1923, Wallace and Ruth, engaged to be married, sailed for Africa with other missionaries. During a short stop over in a missionary home in England, they were anticipating a few moments alone. After the meal one evening, they were seated in the lounge with several others. Various guests left the room. As the last lady went out she said to Wallace, "I suppose you want to say good-night to your fiancee," then walked out and closed the door. But barely a minute later, her head popped back in and she asked, "Have you finished now?"

Skulls and Idols

Landing in Africa they disembarked in Capetown and travelled to a very isolated area called Chavuma in Northern Rhodesia (now called Zambia). A governor once referred to it as the "remotest part of the British Empire." After a long and tiring train journey they arrived at the Victoria Falls. At that time, there were no roads or rail to Chavuma from this point, and the only way to get there was by river. It was a seven week barge trip up the Zambezi river. To the young missionaries it was a fascinating experience. There were so many new and interesting sights to see. Wild life abounded all around. The river was infested with hippopotami and crocodiles. Lions, elephants and other game roamed freely through the countryside.

At last they arrived at Chavuma. Walking up from the river to the proposed mission site, they were horrified to see numerous human skulls, idols and other evidences of heathen practices. This sight left an indelible impression. What impact would the gospel have in this land?

Some months after arriving, Wallace and Ruth were married in Angola, north of Chavuma. In describing their wedding Wallace said, "At the end of the ceremony, the Portuguese officer said something like 'man,' so we decided we must now be married, and have been happily married ever since." They fared better than one missionary who went to the Portuguese officer with his fiancee. Struggling with his limited knowledge of Portuguese, he used the wrong word. Instead of saying, "Will you marry us?" he solemnly asked, "Will you shoot us?"

The wedding cake was made of flour and dried bananas, but what was lacking in ingredients was not lacking in love. The young couple returned to Chavuma where they set up home and united their efforts for the Lord.

Their first home was a hut made from the branches of trees. In place of a door they would put up a barricade of pots and pans to keep the wild animals out.

"The nearest doctor in those days," Wallace related, "was two weeks' journey away. If you were going to get sick, you would have to know at least a month ahead—two weeks to send for the doctor and two weeks for him to come! We would send down the river to civilization for supplies once a year," he would continue. "If you forgot anything one year, you certainly wouldn't the next! We never had just one baby because we started off with twins! We were the first white people that most Africans there had ever seen. One day when I walked into a village, the people ran away. Perhaps you can't blame them for that! You could see them peeking out at us from behind trees.

When my wife appeared, you could see them coming out from the trees to get a better look. However, when they saw our babies, they came right out and one was overhead to say," They must be people because they have children like we do!'"

The people studied him closely to see how genuine he was. They noticed his ability to keep calm in extreme situations and gave him the name of *"Sakuunda"*—"the father of peace." His outstanding quality as a peace-maker was used of God many times, and earned him the respect of many.

Another thing the people noted was the family Bible reading. They were heard to say, "This message he says is from God must be true since he reads the same Book to his family as he does to us. He would not deceive his own children." Wallace had a tremendous respect for the Bible. He would quote, *"For ever O Lord, thy Word is settled in heaven."* This glorious fact ended any controversy in his mind. There was no trying to explain a verse away. He moulded his beliefs around the Word and not the Word around his beliefs. He was a man of the Book. Its pages were searched hour after hour until its message burned within his soul. He simply believed what God had written, taking Him at His Word.

Proving God

When Wallace had left secular work as an electrician with a steady income, it had been a new and not altogether easy experience to live by faith. But God proved that He could be trusted. He experienced the thrill of a life of entire dependence on the Lord for every need. Although the flour barrel was to become very low at times, the Lord never let him down and all his needs were supplied. He describes the following incidents of God's provision of his needs as he trusted Him.

"We were planning a trek to the distant villages to tell the people about God's Son. We very definitely felt that the Lord was leading us to go, but we had one problem. We had no milk to feed our baby twins on the journey. Fresh milk was not available and the nearest grocery store was 600 miles away. But God knew the need. Just the day before leaving, the mail runner arrived. Though scheduled to come every six weeks, he was often unpredictably delayed, as he might be treed by a lion or cut off by flooded plains

"We opened the mail bag, and there to our delight was a five-pound can of powdered milk all the way from Canada. There was also a letter from the sender which read, 'Dear Brother Logan, I was down-town shopping the other day buying milk for my baby when I thought of your twins and wondered if you might be glad of some too. I was planning on mailing it another day, but as I passed by a Post Office right in the store, the Lord seemed to say, 'Why not mail it now.' So I went right to the P.O. counter and mailed you the can of milk. I hope you receive it alright.'

"We praised the Lord for His perfect timing. Supposing she had gone home first and then mailed it several days later; the trip might have been cancelled and many people would not have heard the gospel or been saved. *My God shall supply all your need according to His riches in glory by Christ Jesus.*'

"We were in the midst of constructing the tabernacle at

Chavuma, a building to accommodate 2,000 people, and we had hundreds of employees on the job. In the mail, one day, came a telegram stating: 'All dollar dealings suspended.' This was our first introduction to the depression. I called the workmen and explained the situation, concluding that I would have to put them off till money was available. They replied, 'No, we will finish the job even if we don't get paid.' The work continued, and at the end of the month money was received from Ireland and other parts of the world from people we had never heard of before. When the U.S. dollar had failed, the Lord knew that the Irish money was good! We were able to pay all the workmen, and the tabernacle was completed in three months! *'Great is the Lord and greatly to be praised.'"*

These are just two of many experiences Wallace had of proving God. His exciting exploits in living by faith would fill a book!

Fiery Trials

Pioneering is not easy and the first term had its discouragements and much to dampen enthusiasm. The discouragements Wallace and Ruth faced were enough to send even the most stout-hearted home, but with them, these were to prove their mettle.

Part of everyday living was the inconveniences caused by the lack of "necessities" of life. Courageous Ruth, in setting up home, made do with whatever was available in the bush.

News received of a number of missionaries who had died tragically of tropical fevers in other parts of Central Africa was anything but comforting. Within three years of the arrival of 13 missionaries, only two remained who had not succumbed to black-water fever and other diseases.

Sorrow came to their home too. Grief filled their hearts and tears welled up in their eyes as they helplessly watched the life of their first son, Samuel, only six months old, ebb away with a malignant fever. But God gave such strength that over their baby's lifeless body they were able to say in quiet surrender to His will, *"The Lord gave, the Lord hath taken away; blessed be the Name of the Lord."*

Even the financial success of some of his friends back in the States was used as a tool by Satan to discourage him. Letters arrived telling of Christian friends back home who were now doing very well in business. Some had became managers of banks and other large businesses, were making high salaries and living in beautiful homes. Satan lost no time in telling Wallace that he was wasting his time here in Africa and greatly losing out in life. How cruel Satan can be! But the Lord gently reminded His servant that his pay-day was still coming. God is no man's debtor. *"There is no man that hath left house, or brethren, or sisters, or father, or mother ... or lands, for My sake and the gospel, but he shall receive an hundredfold...."*

Another heavy blow fell. Fred Barnett, a faithful co-worker and friend from Australia, was one day crossing the treacherous Zambezi river near the mission, taking the gospel to outlying villages. The narrow dugout canoe in which he was crossing capsized in the swift current. Since he was wearing his heavy leather boots, Fred did not have a chance. His body was never recovered.

These trials were hard to face, but God gave him courage. He did not rebel when the Lord wanted to teach him lessons. He was quick to accept every circumstance as allowed of the Lord to enrich his spiritual life, which resulted in his developing into a patient, humble and faithful servant of Christ.

White Man, Can You Help Me?

What is it like to witness the work of a diviner? Hear Wallace tell the story in his own words.

"I was treking one day when I came to a place where something had been dragged across the path. Asking one of the carriers what it was, he replied, 'One of evil spirits.'

"'What do you mean?' I inquired. 'Come and see,' was his hushed reply.

"Leaving the foot-path, he led me a short distance into the bush, and there I saw a sight I will never forget as long as I live. On the ground lay a man who had been accused by the diviner of having an evil spirit. They had seized him and held him over a fire, roasting him alive, then dragged him off into the bush leaving him to die in agony. The stench from his burns was so terrible, we could only approach him on the side from which the wind was blowing. Maggots were crawling from his flesh. The sight was nauseating.

"This poor suffering victim of the diviner's cruelty looked up into my face with pleading eyes. In a weak, trembling voice, as a man in desperation looks to his last source of hope, he cried, 'White man, white man, can YOU help me?'

"I could tell from the tone of his voice that others had failed him. Cancelling our plans to go further we made a rough hammock out of the bark of trees and carried him to our mission station where we cared for him. Bandaging his wounds was at times too much for some of us, making us feel ill.

"For months we cared for him. Most of the burns were healing quite nicely, but there was one place on his knee; where the burn was so deep that gangrene had set in. Unable to amputate, we knew that it would be only a matter of time before we would lose him. We told him the story of the love of God and how Christ died for him. One day he said, 'I want that Man to be my Lord and Saviour.'

"Shortly before he died, he called for me and said, `Saku-unda, I'm going to the capitol of God, but before I go, I want to thank you. You have helped me.'

"My thoughts went back to the time I had first seen him lying in the bush and had heard his cry, 'White man, can YOU help me?'"

This experience impressed upon Wallace the value of living for eternity rather than time.

Deadly Poison

The Witch-Doctor crept stealthily along in the darkness. His hand tightly gripped a container of poison. He knew the amount necessary to destroy life, and he had far more than needed. He cautiously approached the Logan house. If he had figured correctly, they would all be out this night to a Bible reading at the home of another missionary.

He drew nearer to the house. He was right. He knew exactly what to do. He stole along to the kitchen veranda where the drinking water was kept. In the darkness he felt for the clay water-pot. His hand found it. Locating the opening, he silently inserted the poison, mixed it well and then vanished into the night. It was now only a matter of time before news of the death of this missionary family would be spreading across the country, then some of his competition would be gone.

While this was taking place, the Logan family were enjoying a delicious meal of fish, followed by a Bible study, in a fellow missionary's home. Not aware of what the witch-doctor had done, they returned home and, thirsty from the meal, made for the drinking water. It tasted slightly different than usual, and after a few sips, they had had enough. The strange taste did not concern them, however, as bad tasting water was not uncommon. They went to bed. During the night they all became violently sick and were too ill even to care for one another; but in the goodness of God, the poison did not take any lives and before long they had all fully recovered.

Shortly after, it was rumored in the neighborhood, "It is no good trying to poison the missionaries, because their God is too strong for our poison!"

Committed

Wallace threw his full weight into the work from the start and did not spare himself. He rose up early and often worked late into the night. He would sometimes say, "I would rather burn out than rust out." He was more than just involved—he was totally committed to a mission for Christ with eternity's values in focus. He was fired with a passion for souls, which no one could quench. In his labor he could say like the apostle Paul, *"so have I strived to preach the gospel, not where Christ was named, lest I should build upon another man's foundation."* His work was done wholeheartedly as unto the Lord.

He believed in the verse, *"by all means save some."* Many recall hearing him proclaim from the platform, "What do you have? Use it for God."

When telling a story, he would dramatize it, really making it live. His congregation did not have a chance to go to sleep! A master of suspense, he held his audience spellbound or, with a surprise move, made them jump as one man. Each story had its direct spiritual application. He was dynamic in his presentation of the gospel and yet down to earth in meeting the needs of his hearers. He would say, "Don't complicate the way of salvation so only the learned can be saved. Don't be hard on a babe in Christ because he doesn't know 'the phraseology,' or because he doesn't know what mature Christians know."

Far more significant than his preaching, was his life. His fellow workers described him as one who was in touch with God, was willing to fit in and *"easy to be entreated"* (Jas. 3:17). A balanced sense of humor enhanced his cheerful disposition. He always showed great respect for older workers, and yet when he himself was old, would so graciously step back to let younger brethren exercise their talents.

Treasures From Darkness

A hush fell across the congregation of 1,800 in the tabernacle at Chavuma. Eyes were riveted on the man who had just walked in. There were whispers, "Do you see who that is?" It was the witch-doctor. But what was he doing here?

While the speaker was still preaching he was abruptly interrupted by the witch-doctor.

"Stop," he commanded.

There was a dead silence. What was he about so say? Everyone waited expectantly.

"Stop! I can wait no longer. I want that Man to be my Lord and Saviour."

In a moment this child of Satan became the child of God. From that day on he was a changed man and lived to prove it by his life. Today, over forty years later, Mwata Sakachama, the former witchdoctor, is still a faithful shepherd and pillar in the church. When antagonists burnt down the meeting house, he encouraged the believers to go on for the Lord. Now they are erecting a new building on the same site.

"A man by the name of Chondela was in the habit of coming late for all the meetings. One day he turned up just as everyone was going out, so I said to him, `Chondela, you remind me of the cow's tail,' and I laughed, but he didn't.

"At the next meeting he was missing. Weeks passed but no Chondela, so I went to look for him. As I came to his village I saw him and greeted him cheerfully, 'Good morning, Chondela.'

'Good morning,' he replied abruptly.

'How are you?'

'Alright,' he retorted sulkily.

'I haven't seen you at any of the meetings lately.'

'You called me a cow's tail and I'm not going to any more meetings.'

'That's just a saying we have, Chondela.'

'I don't care what sayings you have in English. I'm not going to any more meetings.'

'Chondela, come on …' but he was unimpressed.

'I could see I was accomplishing nothing. I had offended him. So I said, `Chondela, I'm sorry I called you a cow's tail, and if you come back to the meetings, I'll never call you a cow's tail again.'

"Chondela came back, and later on trusted the Lord as his Saviour. How thankful I was that God gave me the courage to say, 'I'm sorry.'"

A Hundredfold

On one occasion when Wallace was still a young man, some one came to him and referred to the parable of the sower and the harvest of a hundredfold, then sixty then thirty. He likened the hundredfold harvest to the days of the apostles; the sixty-fold to the time of the reformers, the thirtyfold to the period of revivals around Wesley's time; "nowadays" he continued, "you can hardly expect anyone to be saved!"

Wallace felt discouraged, and later said, "I felt, what was the use of carrying on? We are certainly playing a losing game."

What he did next shows the value of studying the Scriptures for oneself. Grabbing a concordance he looked the passage up. Turning to Mark's account where the order is reversed he read, 44... some thirty fold, some sixty and some an hundred." Jubilantly he exclaimed, "Praise the Lord. I'm going in for the hundred fold!" From that day on he expected big things from God.

The first hundredfold was the joy of seeing his whole family of seven—five girls and two boys—come to Christ at the early ages of five and six. God had blessed the daily family Bible readings. They had paid rich dividends.

The Bible continued to be paramount in the home, even if other things had to suffer. The family altar consisted of more than little "token" readings. An hour or two was spent daily around the open Word.

The whole family attended all the assembly meetings in spite of criticism that this would mean the children's educational loss. Education was never put before the things of the Lord. Wallace and Ruth felt, "What is the use of higher education if it is not used for the Master?" God honored their sincere convictions without being their debtor. Their family now includes two nurses, a doctor, three teachers and a technician, but above this He gave them their life's desire of seeing their entire family saved and serving the Lord.

The first building for services at Chavuma was put up to accommodate one hundred people. The next one seated two hundred. Later on, a building to hold five hundred was constructed. Then the tabernacle was built with a capacity for two thousand people! The need was felt to spread to outlying areas, which resulted in fourteen additional assemblies. A multiplying action took place—people saved, spreading out and witnessing where they went. Today one can meet Christians all over the country who point to Chavuma as the place where they found the Saviour.

Both in Africa and in other continents, buildings were packed out to hear Wallace. He always uplifted Christ. As Wallace and Ruth travelled they prayed and expected to see people saved. Neither language nor race were barriers to them in witnessing. They have spiritual children in many countries throughout the world, for which they gave God all the glory. Thousands of converts can rise up and call them blessed. Thank God Wallace didn't listen to Satan's voice when he told him he was wasting his time. Truly it pays to serve the Lord!

I Am Ready

One of the greatest blessings that comes as a by—product of Christian service is the thrill of seeing what God can do when we yield our lives to Him. Wallace desired to be controlled by the Holy Spirit. He described himself as "only a sinner saved by grace." Realizing this fact, he allowed himself to be pliable in the Potter's hands, and fully surrendered his all to his Master. "God first" was his motto, and this was put into practice even in the smallest details of life. Before making a decision or entering any transaction he consulted his Master. His guide was, *"in all thy ways acknowledge Him and He shall direct thy paths."*

Conscious of human weakness and his complete dependence on God he became a man of prayer, and grew to know his Lord intimately. This deeper prayer life sometimes involved agonizing with tears and other times it was simply the quiet moment by moment communion with God. *"The effectual fervent prayer of a righteous man availeth much."*

There are trials in Christian service but they are allowed for our good, and are never more than we can bear. Wallace had faced many trials. He had been willing to suffer for his convictions even though it could mean death, and was called upon to endure imprisonment, beatings, torture and threats on his life.

Wallace was satisfied to know that he was in the best vocation, with a wonderful Master to serve. When he was young he had put every ounce of energy into the Lord's service. Now that he was older his physical strength was failing, and he was not able to do what he once did. Although now in the sunset years of his life, he did not retire but continued to help out in every way possible. His fellow workers appreciated his foresight. He had weathered many storms. His greying hair was now white. His mind remained lucid, his sense of humor sharp, but he did not waste time in idle talk. He always had time for people and their problems, but not for gossip. One day a group was "hanging up dirty wash" in idle talk. Wallace kept a seal on his mouth. Afterwards one came to him and said, noticed you did not participate in the gossip. I want to thank you for the rebuke and blessing your silence has been to me."

Instead of using criticism, Wallace patiently employed love, prayer and tears. He was slow to express his opinion, but when he did, his words were worth listening to. His godly advice earned him great respect and evidenced that he had experienced many years of walking with his Lord.

He greatly enjoyed the Word. Down through the years the Bible had been his constant companion. Many a time he would study it into the early hours of the morning. Now in the sunset of life, the living Word became all the more precious to him.

He would often pass on a word of encouragement to those around, bringing help and comfort. An expression he liked using when saying good-bye to a young person was, "Be a man for God." Another challenging expression often heard was, "We are not living for time but for eternity."

It seems he had a premonition that his days were now short. "I have no desire," he told me, "to live on simply for the sake of living. When my usefulness is completed, I will be ready to go. I have tried to use my strength for the Lord and I have no regrets."

The last message he gave to his fellow-workers was, "Three cheers from the Bible. *'Be of good cheer; I have overcome the world'* (John 16:33). *'Be of good cheer; thy sins be forgiven thee'* (Matt. 9:2). *'Be of good cheer; it is I'* (Matt. 14:27)."

Toward the end, it was evident from his conversation that he was homesick for heaven and was looking forward to seeing his Lord. Late one Sunday night, February 2, 1969, he had a stroke. Three days later as the sun was setting, this giant for God quietly left this world for his eternal Home.

Instead of his Christian life lasting only two weeks as his old gang had predicted, it had been fifty-three years of happy service for the King of kings.

Telegrams started to come in from different parts of the world. One contained the phrase, "safely landed." One African Christian wrote to the family: "Dear Mother, sisters and brothers in Christ, It was a shock to me when I heard of the death of the father in Christ who has brought us up in spiritual things as long as he was on earth. Nevertheless, I am contented that I will one day meet him up in heaven. Therefore it is up to you and us to live for the Lord as he did. During his stay in Balovale district he has witnessed for the Lord and all the people have seen the Lord in him I have selected a few verses from the Bible for you all to read. May our mighty God comfort you all. Your friend in God."

One elderly blind man who lives not too far from the mission, upon hearing of the death said, "Sakuunda was a righteous man. I know where he has gone, but I'm not going there." Disturbed about his soul, he asked to be led to a local evangelist saying that he wanted to receive Christ as his Saviour.

A Christian Chief, Muwema, a life-long companion of Wallace Logan spoke at the funeral using: *"I am now ready to be offered, and the time of my departure is at hand. I have fought a good fight, I have finished my course, I have kept the faith: henceforth there is laid up for me a crown of righteousness..."*

Fellow missionary, James Caldwell spoke also, using Malachi 2:6, *"He walked with me in peace and equity and did turn many away from iniquity."* Mr. Caldwell said, "I have never been in the presence of Mr. Logan without him eventually turning the conversation to the things of the Lord. . . . Another quality which made him outstanding was his tremendous capacity to forgive."

Another missionary stated, "A suitable epitaph of his life would be, *'I am not ashamed.'"*

The impact of his consecrated life continues to be an inspiration to many to live for their wonderful Lord.

Father

What made him the man that he was,
So patient and gracious and glad,
A man of great love for the lost,
Who gave to the Lord all he had?

What made him leave comfort of home
To toil in a far away land,
That all might share with him his joy
Received from the Father's hand?

He knew that in Christ he had all:
"I've got something better," he'd say.
When asked what it was, he said, "Christ."
He trusted his God day by day.

He treasured and honored God's Word;
The Bible was his great delight.
God gave him great peace in return,
His love and His joy and His might.

—Frances R. Iler (daughter)

A Challenge

Men are being taken in the frontlines of battle, but who will fill the gaps? God is looking for these who will answer the call. The trumpet has blown, the battle is fierce, but where are the men of courage who will come forth to take their stand?

The Gap

A man was taken from the ranks;
But who would take his place?
Would none be found to fill the gap,
To stand before God's face?

The land would have to be destroyed
For want of just one man;
Oh may God find men for the gap
Who'll say, "Through Christ, I can
　　　　　　　—Frances R. Iler

Millions of people in this world are without God and hope. Are we not concerned? Who are our neighbors? Their blood shall be required at our hand.

What are we living for? Are we simply coasting along in neutral without a spiritual goal in life? *What is your life? It is even a vapor that appeareth for a little time, and then vanisheth away.* Will we have nothing to present to the Master?

Every hour, thousands are going into a lost eternity. Does this not affect us? Perishing, perishing but there's no one to tell them of Christ. Can't we hear their cry, *"Carest thou not that we perish?"* Does it leave us unmoved? *"Woe is unto me if I preach not the gospel."* Are we simply making daisy-chains while men and women are falling over the cliff into a lost eternity?

Our Lord said, *"Go ye...."* but who will heed the command? Where are the volunteers?

May our prayer be: Lord, awaken us, stir us, give us a vision and mould us that we might be dauntless for Thee.

"Who then is willing to consecrate his service this day unto the Lord?" Remember, the time is short!

"Only one life, 'twill soon be past,
Only what's done for Christ will last."

Looking Ahead

"What is your life? It is even a vapour, that appeareth
for a little time, and then vanisheth away."

James 4:14

Words and Music by
David and Ruth Ann Logan

In the cool of the eve-ning, when down sinks the sun and gold - en clouds light in the west
At the close of this pass-ing life's short lit - tle day, when all has been done and been said,
"I have fought the good fight and I have kept the faith" Paul said at the end of his life.
Time and strength I now have, but, I must keep in mind; To - day what I let my-self be ...

The bright hues are mem'-ries of deeds that were done when we let God give strength for the test.
and I bid fare-well to this ves-sel of clay, I'll con-sid-er the life that I've led.
But De- mas chose pleas-ures which then loomed so bright his sun-set with sor- row was rife.
When strength has de-parted and ac -tion con - fined is the sun-set to - mor - row I'll see.

P.P.   CRES.

Will my life have a glo - ri - ous sun - set? With a prize when I've fin-ished my course?

DECRES.   P.P.

Or will clouds that are seen at my sun - set, Be but shad-ows of bit-ter re - morse?

Copyright 1967

42

Part 2
Stories and Letters

Early Life

Invitation to Sunday School

"Come to church, Logan." The invitation came from a fellow teenager.

"I can't," responded Wallace, "I don't have a decent suit to wear."

Although his family were members of a mainline denominational church, his exposure to church had been essentially nil. A similar conversation occurred on many a Sunday: "Come to Sunday School, Wallace."

"No, my shoes are too scruffy to go." Or, "I could never go to church in this old shirt."

He did not come from a wealthy family, so fancy clothes were not part of his life. One day, however, he had on a brand new suit, shirt, tie and shoes and he was out strutting his stuff. Too late he saw 'the Sunday school Inviter.'

"Come to church, Wallace."

"Well, my suit isn't... I'd love to but my..." Each potential excuse trailed off dismally. He couldn't escape; there was nothing he could do but go.

As they walked, he lagged behind, hoping still to make a break for it.

No opportunity came. At the young people's class, a German Christian in faltering English taught from Scripture the one and only way to be saved. At the age of nineteen, Wallace trusted Christ as his Lord and Saviour. His life would never be the same.

"The Lord said ... 'He is a chosen vessel unto me, to bear my name'" (Acts 9:15).

A Changed Man

He was a changed man and his new life in Christ was obvious. After his first term as a missionary in Africa, he and his family came back to visit Christians in their home church. One Sunday evening he gave a presentation on the missionary work in which he and Ruth were involved. After the meeting he was at the back of the chapel talking to some venerable, older brethren. Up came a dear brother in the Lord to talk to him. The brother was of limited IQ but the two had been good friends for many years going back to the time before either had trusted the Lord.

"Wallace," he said loudly, "Mr. Smith would like to say hello." For the moment Wallace could not place Mr. Smith and asked who the man was.

Back came the reply loud and clear, "You know him, Wallace, he's the one you stole the tomatoes from!"

"If anyone is in Christ, he is a new creation; old things have passed away; behold, all things have become new" (2 Cor. 5:17).

Didn't I Tell You?

In his teenage years Wallace had two good friends who were brothers. He spent a good amount of time with them. One evening they had been out together and, unknown to Wallace, were now returning past the curfew time that their mother had set for her boys.

Upon arrival at their home, the brothers politely insisted that Wallace go in first. He had just entered the dark living room when from behind the door a shadowy figure appeared swinging a switch which was accurately being landed on his backside. Each swing accompanied the emphasized syllable: "Didn't I tell you not to be late getting home tonight?"

As Wallace tried to dodge the blows, he hollered desperately to her, "It's me! It's me, Wallace! It's me!"

The secret of total Christian unity is found in Philippians 2:5 *"Let this mind be in you, which was also in Christ Jesus."* Our Christian unity should be by alignment of our minds to the mind of Christ. The brothers had good unity of mind with each other, but not with their mother, and their brotherly unity certainly excluded the third member of their group.

Conversion of the Sacher Family

Ruth's mother, Frances Sacher (maiden name Metzger) was born in the town of Niagara Falls, New York, on June 17, 1863. Her husband, Frederick Robert Sacher Sr. was born in Switzerland and immigrated to the States. Thereafter, he married Frances Metzger in Buffalo, New York.

Grandma Sacher was given a Bible to read by her Auntie Diamond who realized Frances was religious, but was not saved. As Grandma read it, she was amazed to read in 1 John 1:7, *"The blood of Jesus Christ His Son cleanses us from all sin."* As a result she trusted the Lord as her Saviour. Thank the Lord for those kinds of 'diamonds' who know the power of God's Word.

Grandma Sacher then prayed for her husband's salvation. When special meetings were coming at the hall, she fixed him his favorite supper and then invited him to the series of gospel meetings starting that night at Elmwood Gospel Hall. He accepted the invitation and through the services he was saved.

After their salvation, the family stopped going to the church which they had been attending previously because the church leader was teaching different things than what they found in the Bible. This leader visited the family because they were no longer attending his church, and told them that they should not be reading the Bible, but that only church leaders should interpret it for them. When it became apparent that the family would not be coming back to his church, he pronounced a curse upon the whole family saying, "You, your children, and your grandchildren will go to hell!"

Later when Grandpa Sacher was dying , the church leader came with one last effort to bring him back into his church and offered to perform the last rites. Grandpa said, "No! It is not necessary since I am depending on the finished work of Christ."

Then the church leader said, "Well, I'll pray the last prayer for you."

"Yes," said Grandpa Sacher, "let's pray," and Grandpa did,

praying that this dear man who had come to see him would come to know the joy of salvation.

A few days after Grandpa Sacher's funeral, there was a knock at the door. This church leader had been so impressed about the peace and the assurance that Grandpa had at the point of death, he came to inquire further about salvation. Grandpa Sacher's son, Paul, led him to the Lord.

Regarding the curse that he had formerly put on the family, all eight Sacher children trusted Christ as Saviour. Among the first generation of descendants in this family: one went to Africa as a missionary, another to China, Indonesia, and Laos, another to Brazil where he served in various capacities including flying for Missionary Aviation Fellowsip. Also among the siblings, Ruth, Paul, Fred, and Joe were great soul-winners. Fred served as Vice President of the Gideons International; he also ran an orphanage, a reformatory, and had a responsible position in an alcohol rehabilitation facility. In all these, he led many to the Lord. Joe also helped Fred with the alcohol rehabilitation center.

Jesus said, *"I have come that they might have life, and that they might have it more abundantly"* (John 10:10). *"The entrance of Thy Word giveth light: it giveth understanding unto the simple"* (Ps. 119:130).

Early African Life

Barge Trips

After arriving by ship in Cape Town, the Logans would take the train up country to Livingstone, Northern Rhodesia (now Zambia).

While on the train between Capetown and Livingstone, after the family Bible reading, six year old Frances asked her father if she was too little to be a Christian. He answered, "the Bible says, *'him that cometh to me I will in no wise cast out'*." (John 6:37)

"I want to come today," little Frances answered, and her twin Esther said, "I don't want to be left out!" They knelt by the train bunks and said, "Lord, we know we are sinners. Please save us today." Ruth wrote down the date—September 2, 1931.

Doubts came to Frances later and she said, "Daddy, do you think I am really saved? I still do so many bad things." He told her that if it depended on what we do, none of us could be saved. He then read Ephesians 2:8-9… *"For by grace are ye saved through faith; and that not of yourselves: it is the gift of God: Not by works, lest any man should boast."* Then he read John 5:24… *"Verily, verily, I say unto you, He that heareth my word, and believeth on Him that sent Me, hath everlasting life, and shall not come into condemnation; but is passed from death unto life."*

"Do you believer that?" he asked.

"Yes," she said.

Then he said, "What do you have?"

"Everlasting life!" she joyfully responded.

Thus, a principle of the family has been underscored. When away from home and the regular schedule of life, continue to be faithful to have the family in the Word of God daily. *"Therefore you shall lay up these words of mine in your heart and in your soul, and bind them as a sign on your hand, and they shall be as frontlets between your eyes. You shall teach them to your children, speaking of them when you sit in your house, when you walk by the way, when you lie down, and when you rise up.*" (Deuteronomy 11:18-19)

After arriving at Livingstone, the family bought supplies for the year that lay ahead.

Then they traveled by a wooden barge on the Zambezi River with 16-20 stalwart African paddlers. The barge was a flat-bottomed vessel approximately 30 feet in length and approximately eight feet in width at the center, tapering in width toward the front and back. The paddlers often would chant in musical rhythm while paddling in unison: "*Kwiya muwato namuchima umwe....Eyo, namuchima umwe.*" "Travelling in the boat with a single heart... Ah yes, with a single heart." The passengers sat in the mid-section which was covered by a rounded canvas canopy. The African captain stood keeping an eye out for danger, and directed the paddlers. Knowing the river well, he would call out orders:

"*Kuchimoswe*" ("To the left") or "*Kuchilyo*" ("To the right") to avoid submerged rocks or sand banks—or hippos.

It took 7 weeks to paddle upstream (and 5 weeks back downstream) to their destination of Chavuma Mission. To negotiate rapids, the passengers would disembark along with their luggage and travel overland by foot. The empty barge would then be paddled, pushed or pulled through the rapids with the aid of long poles to deeper waters where the luggage would be reloaded and the passengers would reembark.

The daily barge travel started early in the morning and ended in time to take advantage of daylight to set up camp. Sunset came around 6:00 p.m. and within a half an hour it would be dark.

During the river trip just after the twins had accepted Christ as Saviour, hippos were encountered, blowing and snorting in the river. One hippo lunged toward the barge—thump!—and tried unsuccessfully to tip it over. The twins commented to their mother, "It's good we've trusted the Lord Jesus as our Saviour, 'cause we didn't have to worry about what the hippo would do!"

Esther continued, "It tried to tip us over, but the Lord Jesus kept us safe and the hippo only bumped its nose."

Frances piped up with, "I am not afraid to die any more, Mother, but that hippo has gone away with a BIG headache!"

As Ruth was preparing to go as a missionary to Africa, one doctor told her, "The crocodiles will eat you!" What actually happened during one river trip was that a crocodile fed her! A hunting crocodile snapped a huge tiger fish in half, with half the fish landing in the middle of the barge. They enjoyed fresh fish for supper!

The Beautiful Zambezi

The beautiful Zambezi blessed with scenery most rare,
To me holds fascination with which nothing can compare.
Let's take a barge trip: There are many sights to see:
Paddlers with a rhythmic tune are rowing steadily.
Amidst the splash of paddles a distant snort we hear
The paddlers change direction lest the hippo comes too near.
A massive, fearsome crocodile lazes on the bank
His toughened hide suggests a mighty army tank.
Beneath our shelt'ring canopy of green we sail along,
Listening to the radiant birds with cheerful, twittering song.
The river takes a bend and grassy plains appear
Where graze the buffalo, the wildebeest and deer.
At eventide the sunset glorifies the west,
Reflecting brilliant colors upon the watery crest.

Penned during another river trip by 16 year old Esther Logan Howell

Upon arrival of the loaded barge at the destination, there on shore would be a crowd of friends and relatives, clapping and welcoming the travelers home with exclamations of joy! Home again!

Traveling to Sakeji School in The Early Days

Wallace and Ruth had a family of seven children; all but one were born in Zambia. Wallace and Ruth were working at Chavuma, Zambia and had to decide "How do we educate our children?" There were no motor roads and therefore no cars, but there were foot paths which Wallace's motorcycle would negotiate. It proved very useful in getting his twin daughters, Frances and Esther, to Sakeji, traveling on the motorcycle's pillion through Angola and then back into Zambia to Sakeji. When Eleanor was ready for school she was put in front on the gas tank and later Viola, the fourth girl, was sandwiched between the twins on a plank behind their father. After a 2 or 3-day journey, everyone arrived safely at Sakeji 300 miles away on a winding footpath - apart from the odd spill. The suitcases, of course, took longer being carried by porters.

But another and more common way of travel to the missionary school was by hammock on the shoulders of faithful men through Angola and back into Zambia to Sakeji. This route took about ten days. The family was growing and Grace, Paul and David had all arrived now. Some of them too enjoyed this form of travel to school.

It involved setting up camp each afternoon. They remember lions roaring when going through the forest and the porters shouting in unison to scare them off. Crossing the flooded rivers, where the bridge was often just a pole was very scary for small children, especially if there were crocodiles in the river below. On one occasion a suitcase fell into the river and when they got across to the other side they found all the contents had been removed from the case by the carriers and were being dried in the sun, displayed so all could see.

Dirt motor roads were finally constructed, linking Chavuma with Sakeji. But even so traveling by vehicle would take four or five days, depending on what time of year it was, and whether or not one got bogged down in muddy roads. In those days one vehicle would pick up many children going to school. Wallace would start off at Chavuma with eight pupils for school, stopping at Balovale to pick up a government official's child and on to Kabulamema and Mutanda for more missionaries' children, landing up with fourteen pupils for Sakeji. .

Today with the CMML Flight Service, Bruce Poidevan and John Loudon can fly school children to Sakeji in just over an hour How times have changed, but the excitement of the previous types of travel was enjoyed just the same.

The family would just like to add how we thank the Lord for the faithful teachers that the Lord has provided for Sakeji down through the years, for the high academic standard achieved and for the basic grounding in the Scriptures given to the pupils.

In Their Own Words

Letter of April 23, 1926

Wallace Logan wrote the following:

I know you will be interested in a few of the details of the itinerating trip Mr. Sims and I have just returned from, so I shall write them as they impressed me.

If I was asked to name this trip, it would be "The Trip of Sorrow," not because of anything that we went through, but because of the condition in which we found the Africans.

When we started we did not look forward to a pleasure trip, for we knew that the flooded rivers and plains were the highest in eighteen years, and mosquitoes not a few.

The first day went nicely, with the exception of being caught twice in rain storms. The second night we were kept awake by the crying and wailing of a young boy, who we found out to be suffering from paralysis. The poor boy has been suffering for a long time unable to move about. The villagers said he cries all night, every night. All we could do was to tell him of the love of God, and pass on. The next day we just reached a village when a little boy of about three years died. The mother of the child had given birth to a baby boy two days before. Our meeting that night was indeed solemn. The Africans at the time of death always sleep outside their huts. Some times they will sleep a month or more outside.

After our meeting, and while we were still in the village, the Africans that were there with us called our attention and said,

"Listen, they are going to make the women drink poison, to see who is the witch that caused the death of the child."

In the raw villages this often happens. A diviner is called to give poison to the suspected ones. And those that die from it are supposed to be guilty for the death. Some having stronger constitutions, are able to throw it up; while the weaker ones can't. Just a few months ago the authorities arrested a group of diviners not far from this place who had given the poison test to some women and over nine died.

We made a big stir, and said we would report them to the Camp, then they started to deny it. The next day, we followed up the man who made the threat and gave him a fright to try to prevent him from carrying out his purposes.

The same day we came across two men who were lepers. Oh my! What a sight: hands, toes, mouth eaten away. They reminded me of some of the worst cases I saw on Leper Island.

We had been walking through so much water, anywhere from ankle to hip-deep and deeper, that we thought to take off our shoes and socks, because they were so heavy in the water. But that night, we did not sleep much for the pain in our legs. The sun had burnt them so that we felt as if hot water was being poured on them. Poor Mr. Sims suffered the most from the after affects, which seemed to cramp his legs, so he could hardly move them after standing still for a moment.

On we went, swimming where we could not walk, and in boats where we could find them. After four days Mr. Sims legs began to get better, and we were not sorry. We found many villages under water. The people carrying sand to build their fires on to keep the fire above the water.

One day stands out in my mind as a day we would not like to repeated frequently. We reached a river crossing at four p.m. After a hard day's trek, thinking we had time to cross, we started, but we found that it took about 45 minutes to cross, and we had thirteen load men carrying tents, food, boxes, beds, etc. We inquired about another boat as the one we were crossing in could carry only one man, without his load and the paddler. They told us we could get another boat about a mile down the river, so with aching legs we started to find the man with the other boats; but we failed and returned by moonlight to find half our loads on one side of the river, and half on the other side. So there we sat with wet clothes, mosquitoes biting, and hunger. No tent, beds or change of clothes. The food box had come, so we got a nice supper started. It was not a pleasant thought to think of crocodiles and hippopotami upsetting the little boat carrying our things. Still we could thank God for the clear moon, our only hope. If clouds came, then what? But God never allows one to be tempted above what they can bear. We had set the table, and just ready to sit down to a much looked for meal when we discovered our table covered with army ants. After clearing them away (which is not always the easiest thing to do) we managed to eat our supper. When we finished our meal, I found they had brought my bedding and set it down on the army ants, so that did not help matters much. After a time, our tents came and we were able to set them up, and make our beds, and the last load came after ten thirty. I may say we did not need to be rocked that night.

While on the way we were able to call on Mr. and Mrs. Hume, where we found them carrying on alone for God, and God's blessing is on their work. We were the first white faces they had seen in over six months. Our short stay with them was one of happy fellowship.

Traveling from there we were reminded once more of the hardships of the road; the first [part of the] night I spent trying to kill mosquitoes. I managed to kill forty in my net, and the rest managed to keep me awake all night, so that I did not sleep a minute.

From there we camped at a place where a mother had just died leaving two young babies behind. And again we preached to the broken hearted in the Chipeshi (death camp).

It was in this village we bought a chicken with some cloth, and later we found the cloth on mahamba (idols representing some dead relations). Upon inquiring, one of our carriers told us that the man who sold the chicken was so glad because of the amount of cloth he received, that he wanted the mahamba to hold it a little while to rejoice his dead relations' hearts, and also to show his thankfulness to them for helping him to get a good price for the chicken.

The next place we slept at we were awakened now and then by an old man who was nearing death's door, and who was crying out every once in a while. We were able to give him a little medicine and then tell him of the One who died that he might live in eternal joys above.

The last day of our journey went quickly traveling through flooded plains where there are no villages. We walked over thirty five miles to our station, and being human it is needless to say we were not sorry to see our wives, children and friends once more.

The trip took eighteen days and we were able to reach over fifty groups of villages and two thousand three hundred twenty-five Africans. The saddest of all is that the majority never had white or black preach to them before. Many begged us to come to build with them. The harvest truly is plenteous and the laborers few.

This letter is so long that I can't say much about our station work. Only let me say, God is hearing your prayer and we see Him working in a wonderful way. Our first meeting place was built for one hundred, then the second for two hundred, and now we are building one for five hundred. Last Sunday we had over five hundred at the Gospel meeting. Two more are asking for baptism.

There are many snakes about these days, but God is keeping us in safety. Recently the chiefess was bit, but she recovered. The same week another man was bit and died the same night. The day before yesterday a large snake came out of my office. And at evening an African was getting some food out of our storehouse and a spitting snake spit at him, but it landed on his arm. If it had spit in his eyes, it might have blinded him. Yesterday we saw one in our yard and when trying to kill it, it turned and chased us; but being ten to one, we were able to kill it. By these things you may know that a missionary needs a powerful God, and a powerful God we have.

P.S. I am enclosing the (or one of the) mosquitoes that just bit me!

Letter of March 23, 1932

Ruth Logan wrote the following:

Mulongesa, an African elder who is in charge of our Chingi out school, was trained for years by Dr. W. Fisher, Mr. Mowat, and Mr. Sims. His gift has been showing itself in various ways and he now has the joy of reaping a rich harvest of souls. Amongst those he has won for Christ is a wicked diviner. She is a real trophy of grace. Her face beams with joy in place of that hard wicked look she had before. I remember Mrs. Sims' fervent prayer for her. Surely! He hears and answers prayer. We also rejoice greatly to see the number who have trusted Christ here on the Chavuma station.

The other day there were thousands of army ants about ten feet from our door step. If the Lord had not brought them to our notice, in no time our house could have been filled with army ants. The only thing we could do then would be to have left the house until they had finished with it. How true is the promise, *"The Angel of the Lord encampeth round about them that fear Him and delivereth them."* We were able to reverse the army by throwing out food in the way we wished them to go. They were traveling five or six abreast with officers at the side and they took three days to pass by.

When Wallace, the children and I were on the Zambezi River, a crocodile followed us to the other side. It was very courageous with head above water most of the time. They usually stay under water following the shadow to the bank and then they give a swift turn, knocking their prey into the river with their tails.

Thanking you for all your prayers; for God is answering, and keeping us from many dangers that we might be living witnesses for Him in this spiritually dark land of Africa. O Lord, keep us shining for Thee until Thy face we see!

Letter of October 8, 1937

Wallace Logan wrote the following:

Recently Mr. Sims, Mr. Geddis, and I started out on a rather unusual trip, which necessitated our traveling under most peculiar and trying conditions. The purpose of the trip was to investigate and explore concerning a suitable place for Mr. Geddis and his family to start Gospel work, in a new district, where no other white people are.

The next day we started off again and everything went alright until we came to a certain swamp. Mr. Sims being first, stepped on what appeared to be a solid place, but it proved to be otherwise and down, down he started to go. Finally, we formed a chain and were able to rescue him. On we went, until once more, we found ourselves in the forest, that was so long and thick, where we had weakened so on the outward journey. This time, we tried to encourage ourselves by saying it is a cooler part of the day etc., but suddenly Mr. Sims' leg gave in and then things looked dark. We generally travel with our carriers, but this was an usual trip and we had to send our carriers to the camp, where we could get water, while we were searching the country etc. Here we were without carriers and a huge forest to go through and one of our number crippled. Mr. Sims is a brick and he struggled through that huge forest, dragging his leg. We were certainly glad to see the camp that night. That evening, we made arrangements for a hammock to be made out of bark of a tree to carry Mr. Sims the next day. As we were now out of the dense bush, we thought we would rush ahead and send for reinforcement from the station to bring in Mr. Sims. When we reached half way, we sat down to have something to eat and when finished, we arranged for food for Mr. Sims, too, when he should arrive. To our surprise, we saw him coming along at a great rate, the hammock was too slow, so he got out and came on all the way with us. He is a brick. The Lord wonderfully made his leg to be as strong as ever.

For some "completion" to the story...

We had several opportunities to speak of God on this journey and the Lord used us to lead a fallen chief back to the Lord.

Heathenism

Witchdoctor's Divining Ball

Wallace came across a crowd of villagers gathered in a clearing in the forest. In the center of the crowd there was a witchdoctor deeply immersed in sorcery to identify the person who had bewitched someone causing the recent death of a fellow villager.

It was their firm belief that sickness and death were not caused by disease but rather as the result of someone surreptitiously bewitching the person who died. Therefore for "justice" to be served, the guilty individual had to be identified and put to death. To accomplish this, the witchdoctor would skillfully work up the emotions of the crowd into a frenzy. Different witchdoctors used various paraphernalia to assist in their divinations. This man had a string, one end of which was tied to the branch of a tree; then the string went through a spherical seed pod about the size of a golf ball. The other end of the string he held in his hand. When he threw the ball upward on the string, if it slid back down on the string, the answer to his question was "No" but if however it stayed up on the string, the answer was "Yes."

To identify the believed perpetrator, the witchdoctor had to find the appropriate evil spirit to provide the information. He would call out a name as he tossed the pod upward "Kayongo, Kayongo." The ball slipped down each time Kayongo's name was called. No, it wasn't Kayongo who could help him. Up the string the pod went again, "Chivumina, Chivumina." Down came the ball. He repeated this procedure with the names of other evil spirits. Suddenly the ball for no visible reason stuck at the top of the string when he named one spirit. "Or is it another spirit?" down came the ball "No." He now had the spirit identified.

Calling upon this spirit to guide him, he asked, "Is the guilty person here?" The ball stuck at the top of the string: "Yes." Then one by one the witchdoctor called out the names of the people in the crowd around him. "Is the bewitcher Sambongo?" The ball slid down: "No." Sambongo breathed a sigh of relief. "Is the guilty person, Nyakananga?" The sliding ball gave the answer "No."

Finally he came to an elderly individual—usually the accused was an older person who could no longer take care of himself and thus was a burden to society.

"Is Satema the one who bewitched our dead friend?" There was a hushed silence! The ball stuck! "Or is it some other person?" the ball slowly slid down the string. Tell me again, "Is it Satema?" the ball clung to the string. Satema it was. His face was ashen with fear. The crowd was about to leap upon him and drag him off to his doom. The witchdoctor was hurrying to put away the tools of his trade when Wallace stepped into the clearing. "Give me that ball" he said firmly, his sudden appearance and authoritative voice taking everyone by surprise. "No," said the witchdoctor, "if you touch it you will die." In the strength the Lord gave him, Wallace replied, "I don't care." Then he did what only a foreigner could have done and got away with it, he wrenched the divining ball out of his hand.

Mechanically minded, Wallace had an idea of how the thing worked. Then he took a few moments to verify its function. "You sit there," he told the witchdoctor. He threw the ball up on the string then pointing to the witchdoctor asked, "Is this man telling the truth?" The ball slid down the string. "No." "Or is he deceiving the people?" the ball stuck, "Yes." "Is he a good man?" "No." The crowd gaped in astonishment.

Although a large crowd was present Wallace knew that if he announced that he would show the trickery the next day, far more people would come. "Tomorrow, when the sun is at this position (pointing to high noon) I will show you how this man has been deceiving you." The next day at the appointed time, well over a thousand people came.

Wallace tied one end of the string to a tree branch, instructed the ball to respond to his questions about the Witchdoctor's truthfulness, and amazed the crowd. He then showed them how it worked. "You see this round seed pod? It's covered with dark wax so you can't see inside it. The string goes through the pod from holes placed on opposite sides of the ball. Inside the ball, the string goes by an off-center reed, so that when one pulls on the string it binds on the reed keeping the ball up. When the string is loosened, the pod slides down. In this way the witchdoctor has been wrongly accusing people of bewitching others. Many in the crowd were very angry remembering how innocent relatives of theirs had been destroyed due to this man's trickery.

This was the opportunity Wallace wanted to reach all those gathered with the Gospel. Holding up a Bible, he read to them John 3:16 in their language. When you say to us, "Let me see that," we don't reply, "No, no, you can't touch this or you'll die." You see this has no wax covering but it is an open book with a special message from God in heaven. That was the start of many turning to the Lord and being brought out of darkness into His marvelous light.

Many years later, shortly before his homecall to heaven, Wallace, Ruth and Grace visited an assembly a few miles away from Chavuma Mission. After the breaking of bread an older man who had been sitting right next to Wallace came up to him and said, "Sakuunda, do you remember coming across a crowd of villagers gathered in the forest listening to a witchdoctor who was 'smelling out the witch' who had caused a death? Do you remember taking away his divining ball right out of his hand?" "Yes, I remember it very well," replied Wallace. "Well I am that very witchdoctor. I ran away from you that day because you were exposing my sorcery and trickery. But the Lord found me, saved me and delivered me from witchcraft." What a joy it was for Wallace to sit next to his new-found brother in Christ and with him remember the Lord together: a foretaste of Heaven! *"Cast thy bread upon the waters, for thou shalt find it after many days"* (Eccl 11:1).

Letter of May, 1964

Wallace Logan wrote the following:

Recently we buried an ex-diviner. Some of you may remember seeing the divining ball which I showed on furlough many years ago and which I had taken away from a diviner. The other day this diviner died. The story is this. Some years after I had exposed his divining to the whole countryside his younger brother trusted in Christ and then led the diviner to the Lord. The diviner in turn led others of his relatives to the Lord until now many of them are saved and at the Lord's Table. He bore a wonderful testimony right up to the minute he died. The whole countryside is talking about his life and death and the great influence for God he was.

You're Sitting on my god!—A Cultural Faux Pas

On a walking gospel safari, Wallace arrived in a remote village and, being weary from the journey, he sat down on what appeared to be a wooden stool. No sooner had he done so, than an agitated man came running over saying, "You're sitting on my god!" It was not a stool but an idol the man had made for him to worship. Wallace stood up, apologized for what he had done in ignorance then quietly said to the idol worshiper, "You shouldn't have a god that can be sat on."

Wallace went on to tell the man and his fellow villagers about the One True God, the God Who made heaven and earth; the God who loves us so much that He sent His Son to die for our sins.

"He cuts down cedars for himself,...it shall be for a man to burn, for he will take some of it and warm himself;...he burns half of it in the fire; with this half he eats meat;...and the rest of it he makes into a god, his carved image. He falls down before it and worships it, prays to it and says, 'Deliver me, for you are my god!'....and no one considers in his heart, nor is there knowledge nor understanding to say, 'I have burned half of it in the fire, yes, I have also baked bread on its coals; I have roasted meat and eaten it; and shall I make the rest of it an abomination? Shall I fall down before a block of wood?" (Isa. 44:14-19).

"And there you will serve gods, the work of men's hands, wood and stone, which neither see nor hear nor eat nor smell" (Deut. 4:28).

Grave Watchers

A prominent chief had just died. His slaves were terrified, and for good reason.

"In years past, when an important chief died, his slaves were taken, one was killed and put at the bottom of the grave and the body of the chief was laid on top of the slave's body. Another slave was killed and placed on top of the chief's body. The earth was then filed in and ten or more slaves were killed. Their blood was used to make a mud with which to plaster on top of the grave! The rest of his slaves (possibly a hundred or more) had their arms and knees broken and they were placed around the grave where they died in agony. They were called grave watchers."

On one occasion a grave watcher, named Chikunga, managed to escape by painfully dragging himself to safety. Eventually he recovered, but without medical care to set the broken bones, his arms and legs were left with considerable and permanent deformity. In addition, following his harrowing experience he had major speech deficit and he had to resort to making hand gestures to make himself understood. Sometime later he made his way to the Chavuma area. He heard the good news of salvation through Christ and accepted Him as Saviour, and was later baptized.

Although physically crippled he was gloriously liberated from spiritual slavery. When asked if he knew the Lord, he would point to his heart, then pointing upward, his face would light up with a radiant smile. There was no question about the joy that Christ had brought into his life.

Sent *"to preach the gospel to the poor; to heal the broken-hearted, to preach deliverance to the captives, to set at liberty them that are bruised"* (Luke 4:18).

"Show forth the praises of Him who hath called us out of darkness into His marvelous light" (1 Pet. 2:9).

Some Tribal Customs

Height of a Child Used Instead of Age

In former times, no record was kept of consecutive years; hence, the age of an individual was not known. The height of a child would be indicated by the height of a horizontal arm. Unwitting offence could occur by using the wrong gesture to refer to the height of a child. "Is your child this tall?" accompanied by the open hand, palm down, is an insult. The hand held horizontally with the palm facing downward is used to denote the height of an animal. For indicating the height of a human, the wrist is bent fully upward and the open hand with gently curved fingers held vertical to the arm (as if being held behind the child's head).

Etiquette

To be polite in receiving anything by hand, one should never take it with just one hand. Either both hands are extended to receive whatever is being given or one hand forward and the other hand touching the arm midway of the extended hand.

A Knock at the Door

Instead of a knock at the door to announce one's appearance at a house, one would clap their hands at the door outside. Sometimes before the clap is given, peeking into the curtainless window of the house would be done to see if the person is there!

Africa, Man's Paradise

There is a saying that "Africa is a man's paradise!" Why would it be called a man's paradise? Well, in walking on a journey, the wife often carries a young child tied on her back, another child in her arms and everything they are taking with them bundled and balanced on her head. The man with his walking stick, walks in a position of importance in front of her, never behind. With a twinkle in his eyes, Wallace would often be heard to say, "Africa is a man's paradise, and I'm going back!"

Attractive Teeth

In times past one of the customs which was not infrequently done, was chipping the teeth to make them pointed. One might wonder whether or not the pain of the chipping of one's teeth was worth it. Those who followed the practice would respond with a resounding "yes", in view of the resulting beautiful appearance!

Twins

When twins are born, one of them must be immediately destroyed. Also, if a baby has the upper teeth come through first, that young child must be destroyed; custom dictates it can be accomplished by throwing him into the river. We don't need to ask why the Lord planned that the first of Wallace's and Ruth's children should be twins and the upper teeth of one of them would come through first! This was a very graphic illustration for those who had grown up with the practice to show that Believers in the true God did not do it. Wallace and Ruth did not follow the heathen custom, but rejoiced in God's gift to them of twin girls and lovingly brought them up in Christ's love. By this they showed the preciousness of each life from God. These same twins later became both trained nurses and midwives. In the medical work at Chavuma, their training helped to save many a life and safely deliver babies including many sets of twins. Most of all they witnessed to many patients of the wonderful salvation through Jesus Christ the Saviour.

In considering some of the heathen customs one must remember that cruel customs can be found among people of ALL races and the need for "the light of the glorious gospel of Christ, who is the image of God, to shine unto them."

In Their Own Words

Letter of February, 1942

Wallace Logan wrote the following:
Satan is not idle either. Where God works, Satan works also. But "Greater is He that in you, than he that is in the world ."

One night about 2 a.m. an African came to our bedroom all excited and said, "Come quickly they want to kill Sambaulu" (He is an evangelist whom God has used mightily to establish and build up a happy African church at one of our out stations). We dressed and went, but only to find him burnt out of house and home. Everything gone, even the meeting house. He was awakened by the noise of fire and found a hole burning in the roof. It appeared as if someone had thrown a burning grass torch on the thatch. It looked like an enemy had done it.

While the flames were devouring his house and life-time belongings, with hundreds gathered, he and his wife sang, "I have a house eternal in the country of God." One was heard to say, "The believers are different, they are singing, we would be reviling."

It was later discovered that the door of their house had been tied shut in order to bar their escape. Thank the Lord that they had constructed their house with a window, something that very few Africans had, and they were able to escape through the open window.

Letter of November 25, 1964

Wallace Logan wrote the following:

While on the other side [of the Zambezi River] we came across a very sad case of heathendom. A woman had just given birth to a stillborn.

About one hour later, while the woman was in an extremely weak condition, her very own mother gave the daughter a tremendous beating for not giving birth to a live baby. Such cruelties are daily happenings in heathendom. Truly we need to reach them more quickly with the love of God.

Another place we visited was known for its witchcraft - a stronghold of Satan. We felt we needed the whole armor of God there. A short while before, a diviner had put a half crown (about 40 cents) on the ground and told the people that whoever touched or took the money would die. For days no one went near it. Then a Christian hearing about it went directly to it and called a crowd together and said, "Just to show you that Christians have no fear of the spirits I'll take it." He picked up the coin, put it in his pocket and then went off. I told a large crowd that if ever they saw another half crown or £1 note to let me know! Much laugher followed! It pleased God to give us liberty in the messages. Much power was felt and some professed faith in Christ. It encouraged the little assembly there which was started through the faithful work of the Lukolwe brethren.

The Lunda paramount chief, who is a Christian in fellowship, has asked us to bring the Gospel Bus for the opening of the new meeting place for the assembly at their capitol. He has told me that the elders there want me to officially open this hall. We thank God for this because this is a Lunda work and I speak Luvale. Three years ago the two tribes were quarreling. Now they are together and the Lundas have asked me (a Luvale speaker) to open their new meeting place. Praise the Lord! (Eph. 2:14).

Vision to Reach People with the Gospel

The Gospel Bus

Wallace, with the encouragement of Ruth, was a man of great vision. He was constantly on the lookout for something which might generate interest in the gospel. Where some might see potential problems, Wallace would usually think about how something might be used for spreading the good news of salvation. He would prayerfully ask the Lord for guidance and wisdom as he thought of new ways to reach out to others with the Word of God.

He regularly used stories and everyday objects to illustrate spiritual truths, following the way the Lord preached. In this way he was often able to gather a crowd who would listen to him preach.

With a burden to reach out further afield from Chavuma Wallace and Ruth prayed about how they could get to more distant villages and other areas and even to the cities with their dense populations and possibly into adjoining countries. Wallace began to think about converting a school bus with basic living facilities in which they could travel and reach people in these areas. Much prayer went up about it asking the Lord that if this was His will He would provide it.

Christians in North America heard about the School Bus project and wrote asking more about it. Dave Madsen, with his plumbing business, and other friends from the Lansdowne assembly in Philadelphia started to spear-head the project. First a school bus was selected and the color changed from yellow to green! It was wonderful to see how friends from all over worked together to provide a fully equipped mobile home including two bunk beds, stove, cupboards, shower, toilet and a tent attached to either side for more sleeping accommodation, and a dining facility. There was storage on the top of the bus for luggage and other equipment.

When they sailed from New York City in 1953, Wallace and Ruth with their seven children headed to Cape Town, South Africa and on board was the completed Gospel Bus ready for its new work in Africa. And what a wonderful send-off from fellow believers at the New York docks.

It was a long drive from Cape Town through Southern Rhodesia, to Northern Rhodesia and on one occasion a motorist flagged them down. The driver got out his car and said to Wallace, "I'm sorry to delay you but I thought we could compare notes as I also run a circus!"

Finally back at Chavuma, the Gospel Bus was a great help in reaching many of the outlying assemblies, enabling the to preach the gospel and to encourage the Christians in their walk with the Lord. At one place after a visit had been made, a heathen woman tested the faith of her newly saved husband by brewing him a nice pot of beer. She set it before him on a sweltering hot day, but to her amazement he said, "Take it away for I am now a Christian." After she watched him for a few weeks she came one day came and said, "I also want to accept, my husband's Saviour."

Wallace and Ruth received many requests both from mission stations and the local assemblies and villages to visit them and hold gospel meetings. Their desire was that the Gospel Bus would be used to encourage missionary brothers and sisters on other stations, and also to strengthen the local assemblies. As a result of these visits many turned to the Lord and new assemblies were started. Something that brought much joy was the happy fellowship and spirit of love among the local groups of Christians. *"By this shall all men know that you are my disciples if you have love one for another"* (John 13:35).

Once when they were visiting a village where the Gospel Bus had been three years before, they found a little group of Christians going on well for the Lord. Two evangelists spoke to a man who had been saved three years before and appeared to be going on brightly. To their amazement however they saw a fetish outside the door of his hut! When he noticed their surprise he quickly said, "This is not my fetish. It's my wife's." The evangelists prayed about it and felt they should mention what a poor testimony it was for a Christian to have a fetish at the entrance of his house.

When they later returned they rejoiced to see that the fetish was gone and he said, "I am a true lover of God and after you left I felt that others too might think that it was mine so I have destroyed it." However while they were still talking, his wife returned from the field, noticed her fetish gone and angrily went inside the house. Her husband followed her in and in a low voice spoke to her. She started shouting at him, "I refuse to live with you." But when he tried to talk quietly to her she rushed out of her house and into a neighbor's house saying, "I'm leaving him and going to my relatives."

The evangelists came to Wallace wondering what to do. Wallace questioned the wisdom of the husband's action. For, after all, to take away another's idols is not the duty of a Christian. If the owner does not have something better to take their place forcing the issue will not help that one.

Ruth had gone that day to the station for supplies expecting to return the next day. Wallace prayed with the evangelists asking God to show them what to do. One evangelist said to him, "If Nyakuunda (Ruth's African name) were here, perhaps she could help. She knows how to handle people well. " To his great delight Ruth returned unexpectedly the same day. They related the quarrel to her. Ruth then contacted the woman and asked her if she would make some nice mush for their supper. The woman came to the Bus with the mush and that evening she also came to the meeting and sat next to Ruth. That night Ruth had the joy of leading her to the Lord. The quarrel was now settled – husband and wife were rejoicing together in the Lord – the fetish gone! Praise the Lord! The value of asking a favor of the one you are trying to win for Christ is known to many soul winners.

On one occasion they had an opportunity to visit the palace of the paramount chief and to stay several days with the Gospel

Bus preaching the gospel.

At a mission station to the south, they were invited as a family to visit and had the joy of seeing over fifty turn to the Lord. More trusted Christ after they left.

Another invitation came from Calunda, Angola, where Mr. and Mrs. Nigel Arnot labored. The Lord blessed and a number professed to be saved. Then they went with the Gospel Bus to Kavungu, where Mr. Albert Horton and his wife worked. Over 100 professed to be saved and they wrote later to say how encouraged the missionaries had been and that some of the new converts were giving them great joy in that they were reaching out to others and sharing what Christ meant to them.

After the Angolan trip we started to travel further afield to Kitwe on the Copperbelt where about 5000 people attended the meetings. The Lord helped in controlling the crowds and the people listened well to the messages. The theme song was put into the language and dialect of the people being visited at each place. Interpreters were helpful in each new area visited.

In Their Own Words

Letter written February 27, 1954

Wallace Logan wrote the following:

It was a joy to hear the Gospel being preached by Paul, Bob (Young) and David as well as by Mr. Sims and John (Sims). One could feel the Holy Spirit's power as the messages went forth. One day after the Gospel went forth with great power by the mouths of several witnesses for Christ, it was interesting to see Mother, Frances, Esther, Eleanor, Viola, and Grace all busily engaged talking to interested souls. Paul had just led one to the Lord when Bob came and said, "Is this not a grand sight to see people being led to the Lord wherever you look?" Just then a man came to me and said, "I want to accept the Lord Jesus as my Saviour."

My, how handy the Gospel Bus is! If it were not for the Gospel Bus we would not be able to reach these distant villages. On practically every trip we go with it, souls profess to be saved. Those who have made it possible and are praying for us in the use of it will rejoice one day when they see how God has used the Gospel Bus.

God has greatly blessed the work here at Chavuma and the large supply of flannel graph material and other things given to us while on furlough are now being used of God to win many. God is hearing your prayers; pray on and share the blessing.

Letter of November, 1954

Wallace Logan wrote the following:

Some time ago we took the Gospel bus to a district where Jehovah's Witnesses had a stronghold and after a few days of preaching the Gospel many came out for the Lord. Just recently we had the joy of baptizing some of them and a little assembly is about to be started in that district.

The other Sunday several professed to be saved here at Chavuma and we went out into the distant villages with the Bus after the meetings here, and several others came to the Lord in surrounding villages. We stopped at a village where God has been working. Two youths came to know the Lord. The headman of that village was saved a week or two before this. There are now 16 professing Christians there. It was a joy to hear them tell of how they had led one of their neighbors to the Lord during the week.

I have just recently had the joy of baptizing over 20. One was the Prime Minister, or spokesman for the headman of the district, where the new assembly is about to be started, as a result of the Gospel Bus visit. Another was a blind man. His face lit up as he came out the waters of baptism. After the baptism we took the Gospel Bus to a distant village and several hundred people gathered to hear the Gospel and that night four came to us and said they wanted to accept Jesus Christ as Saviour. The next day two more came out for Christ and we have received word to say that since coming back God is speaking to many there. We expect one day in the not too far future there will be a little assembly there as there are quite a number of Christians there now.

We have received many other calls from both mission stations and African assemblies and villages and shall try to get out to them as the Lord enables us. Please pray and share the blessing, and keep the Gospel Bus rolling. Our desire is that the Gospel Bus may be used to encourage our missionary brothers and sisters on other stations and to help our African assemblies by systematically visiting them, and also to reach unsaved in the distant villages.

We specially ask your prayers for an unusual opportunity in the capital of the Paramount Chief. It the Lord enables us we would like to take this trip in the near future and stay several days with the Gospel Bus in that district.

There is another item for which we would appreciate your prayers and that is, for many years the people on the west side of the Zambezi River have been asking us to open up a mission station there. We have now been able to send in an application for a mission site and it has met with the approval of the local chiefs and we expect Lord willing, to get some building built there immediately. We are expecting the Lord will send out new workers from the homeland but until such time we are hoping to man the station from our Chavuma staff, which will be an extra strain but, *"As thy days so shall thy strength be,"* so we will lay hold on this promise.

On our way over to make out the above-mentioned site we came across a group of women with gourds and basins and upon inquiring found out that they were miles from home in search of hairy caterpillars for their pots! We asked them if they were without meat for their pots and they replied that they had meat in the village but had a special hunger for caterpillars so were out in search for same.

A few weeks ago when I was over 600 miles away from Chavuma, I stopped at a mining district and it was a joy to break bread with an assembly there entirely run by the Africans, and found about a score of men and women who had been saved at Chavuma and were in fellowship here.

They are now in this African assembly at the mine. It is good to see them spreading out into other districts and assemblies starting.

Another thing that greatly encourages us is the happy fellowship and spirit of activity that is among the local African assemblies. Three of these assemblies have work started in distant villages, and several have been saved through their efforts and the possibility of assemblies being started in the near future as a result of their evangelization is very great.

So dear ones, continue to pray and help us to keep the Gospel Bus going and then in the coming day we shall rejoice together.

Letter of November, 1956

Wallace Logan wrote the following:

The Gospel Bus certainly draws the crowds. Without it we used to go into a village, invite the people to come to the meeting, and all would agree to come, but if ten percent of those invited came one would feel well paid for the effort. Now with the Bus, we only need to stop it for a few minutes and the people gather by the hundreds.

On this trip we passed through a government boma (post) and within two hours we had our camp set up for the night and over 1000 gathered for the meeting, including government messengers and school students, policemen, teachers, etc. A large number came to us after the meeting and expressed their desire to accept Jesus Christ as Saviour. At another place many Europeans came, including the government officials and the doctor and nurses of the local hospital.

We showed pictures of the life, death, resurrection and coming again of the Lord. Many in these parts have never seen anything like them.

Some would come to us after the meeting and say, "We have heard with our ears about Jesus Christ, but now we have seen with our eyes of Him might works in helping people and dying for us. It has now entered our hearts and we want to accept Him as Saviour."

One cripple, after seeing a picture of a pair of crutches, and having been told that these would be left behind after the Lord comes, if they were owned by a Christian, came to us and asked, "Do you mean that if I accept the Lord Jesus I won't need to walk with crutches in heaven?" We told him that all suffering was due to sin having entered the world. Christ came to save from sin and to take us to a happy country that knows no sin or suffering. He replied, "Tell me more and how I can receive Him." This we did and I wish you could have seen his joy as he limped away with his crutches, rejoicing in his new-found Saviour and the happy prospects of one day living without crutches. If you could have seen just him, even without the many other cases of men, women, and children who were saved you would feel well repaid for any part you have had in making this Gospel Bus possible, or helping it to reach the thousands that are perishing in the land of Central Africa. Many Christian wives saw their husbands saved, Christian husbands saw their wives saved, for whom they had been praying, and in other cases families were completed as the last members turned from heathen darkness to the light of the glorious Gospel. Pray on dear ones. We shall try to be faithful in taking the Gospel out, amid many hindrances, trials and oppositions.

Letter of December, 1963

Wallace Logan wrote the following:

This year owing to the pressure of the work on the station we were later than usual in getting the campaign started. Some meetings were affected by rain and the lights attracted "millions" of insects. They got into our ears, eyes, noses, mouths and into our food and down our backs! They made it anything but comfortable for us. But it is an ill wind that blows no one any good. Many of the Africans rallied under the lights and scooped them up by the basins full for their pots.

We had just started the meeting one night when it began to rain. So we said to the crowd gathered, "The rain has come so we had better stop." It was our last night in the district. The people called out, "No, don't stop we will stay." We went on with the meeting. The rain came down much heavier and again we suggested closing. They again called out for us to continue. We asked, "What in pouring rain like this?" They said, "Yes." So we continued with the rain pouring down and the people stuck it out for over an hour. I have never in my life seen anything like it. After the meeting was over and the people gone we noticed a man sitting up against a tree – sound asleep! The rain still pouring! Evidently it turned out to be like a usual meeting even with the odd one here and there asleep! Even as the apostle Paul experienced in his meeting. (Acts 20:9).

Then invitations were coming in from other countries to the north—Congo, Burundi, and Rwanda. So an extensive trip was planned to visit these countries.

The first stop in Congo was Elizabethville (Lubumbashi) with an opportunity to reach crowds each day between 5000 and 10,000 with the good news of God's love and salvation. Traveling on north visiting mission stations on the way going as far as Nyankunde with Bill Deans and the many missionaries there, on to Lolwa with the Spees and those working with the pygmies, and then into Burundi and Rwanda visiting Carl and Eleanor Johnson and family. The Lord blessed – many heard the gospel for the first time and many responded and handed their lives over to the One Who died for them. The Lord be praised too, for the safety He gave over the thousands of miles traveled over many rough roads and high mountain passes.

God certainly used the Gospel Bus. As we write, it has been "retired" to a Mission Youth Camp site where it being used as sleeping quarters for camp counselors.

Letter of January 15, 1955

Wallace Logan wrote the following:

Recently we visited a group of villages on the other side of the Zambezi River. A few weeks before that the headman came out for the Lord and has been a real testimony in that district. The heathen have been anxiously watching him to see if he is going to stand for Christ.

Well the Lord has strengthened him and now there is a fine group of believers that are going on well for the Lord. They have had much joy in leading some of their own neighbors to the Lord recently.

At the river crossing, we were met by some of these Christians who then led us into the forest along a winding native foot path. They told us that they had now made a place for holding meetings and for worshiping God. This, of course, greatly rejoiced our hearts. We then came to a clearing in the bush, where forked branches had been placed vertically in the ground and other branches laid across to make primitive seats. Other logs were placed in a row on the ground to provide more seating capacity. The news of our arrival spread and in less than 10 minutes a crowd of 50 villagers had gathered and we had the joy of preaching the Gospel to them and also passing on a word of encouragement to the believers.

Letter of January, 1965

Wallace Logan wrote the following:

Many years ago while traveling in Central Africa we came across a white man and his wife, Mr. and Mrs. Colliass, who were working for a European trader about 300 miles from here. I spoke to them about the Lord and the meaning of salvation and they both accepted the Lord Jesus Christ as their Saviour. In due course they were baptized and received into church fellowship. A number of years ago they came to work for Mr. B. P. Rudge, a Christian trader at Balovale, 52 miles south of us. They both have been a great help in the African church there.

Recently the widowed sister of Mr. Colliass and her son Ronnie, who is 17 years old, came to live with them from South Africa. Ronnie came to visit us at Chavuma a couple of weeks ago. After talking to him about the Lord and pointing out to him his need of Christ, he kneeled and accepted Christ as Saviour. A few minutes later he said, "I have been going to church all my life but no one has ever showed me these things before. He was so happy and full of joy in his newly found Saviour. He went back to Balovale the next day and said to his mother, "Mother, I have been saved." Before he could get any further his mother said, "And so have I." Their joy was indeed full.

His mother, the day after Ronnie had been saved, had been with Mr. and Mrs. Colliass, who are now in business for themselves as building contractors. They were taking stock at one of their stores about 120 miles in another direction, when Mrs. Colliass spoke to Ronnie's mother about the Lord and she too took Christ as her personal Saviour.

So mother and son met (not knowing what had happened to each other) to announce to the other that the Lord had saved them. Mrs. Drew, Ronnie, and the Colliasses have just spent

Christmas with us and when they left they told us that it was the happiest Christmas they had ever had.

I sat down with Mrs. Colliass while they were here and said to her, "Mrs. Colliass, I would like you to tell me what happened and what you said to your sister-in-law when she trusted Christ." She replied, "I just used the verse that you gave me when I trusted the Lord many years ago - John 3:16." How nice to know that John 3:16 is still powerful in bringing many souls to Christ. In conversation with Mrs. Colliass it was mentioned that Mrs. Colliass being my spiritual child it would make Mrs. Drew my spiritual grandchild." A big smile came to her face and she said, "What is Ronnie to Mr. Logan?" Truly we are one big spiritual family. Let us all go on winning more for our altogether lovely Lord and Saviour Jesus Christ.

The story does not end here. Mrs. Drew wrote to her married daughter in South Africa to tell how she had received the Lord and how happy she was. Her daughter wrote back, "Pray for me. I too feel I need that, for there is something missing in my life." We are all praying now for her and her husband that the Lord will save them. Please join us and share the blessing.

Letter of January, 1961

Wallace Logan wrote the following:

Lord willing, Paul and I with two African elders will revisit every place where we have preached, this time not so much in a Gospel effort, but to build up the professors.

Water Won't Run Uphill

Malaria took a high toll of human life in the early days. Because it was noted that malaria occurred more frequently in low lying regions, Chavuma Mission was built on a 300 foot high hill. A half mile from the Mission, there is an abundant water supply, the Zambezi River.

To get water for Mission use people would be paid to carry it. A hollowed out gourd, or calabash, would be filled at the river. This was placed on the head and then, hands free and with superb balance the African would walk to the top of the hill.

When the Mission's water needs increased, the Lord supplied a diesel powered pump along with enough 2 inch diameter metal pipe to reach to the top of the hill. As Wallace was working on it, local people would come by. "What are you doing, Sakuunda?" "I'm putting a pipe together to carry water from the river up to the Mission." "But water doesn't run uphill," they would patiently explain. "If you had a lake on top of the hill, you could get water to run down to the river. But water won't run UP hill." Wallace would explain that he had a pump to pump it up. "We don't care what you have, water doesn't run UP hill."

Wallace was a man of vision—the Lord had given him the ability to see opportunities to attract more people to hear the Gospel. And here he saw just that—a possible opening to gather a crowd to use the chance to give a lesson from Scripture. After he had everything hooked up (but before he tried it out) he announced that on a certain day "when the sun is like that" pointing straight up with his hand, indicating high noon, they could see water run UP hill. So that all could see the event, he placed the end of the open pipe some six or eight feet in the air.

The Luvale people have a symbolic hand sign consisting of a token spit between thumb and forefinger. The forefinger of the other hand is then placed where he spat. The gesture means, "You said that there are six digits on a hand. You're wrong, there are only five!"

On the designated day, an immense crowd gathered expectantly. Wallace gave the signal to start the pump a half a mile away and they waited for the water to arrive. And waited.... And waited.... And waited.... He noticed several people furtively spitting between thumb and forefinger. A full half hour went by; no water.

All of a sudden the water gushed out—apparently it had taken that long to fill a half a mile of pipeline. People went wild, dancing with glee in the flowing water. When they had settled down, he told them about the living water that Christ gives. They heard about the good news of Salvation from John 4.

Cripples' Day

"Then He also said to him who invited Him, 'When you give a dinner or a supper, do not ask your friends, your brothers, your relatives, nor rich neighbors, lest they also invite you back, and you be repaid'" (Luke 14:12).

After reading this, Wallace suggested "Cripples' Day."

A special day was organized at Chavuma for the elderly and cripples of the area. Very little love and kindness is shown to them in the villages by unsaved relatives, and often their demise is arranged with the witch doctor by children who don't want to feed or be burdened with them any more.

Cripples' Day was a busy one for all. A good quantity of food had to be prepared, used clothing sent from overseas laid out, and speakers arranged to give them the Gospel.

On the day preceding Cripples' Day, a vehicle with a loud speaker was driven through the villages, heralding the invitation to all the elderly and cripples.

"Tomorrow, a truck will come to pick you up and take you to Chavuma hill for the day. You will be given food, clothing, gifts, and a happy time. Then in the evening , the truck will take you home again."

A few of the seventy or more of our scantily clad guests, the lame, halt, blind, and lepers, had to be lifted up onto the bed of the truck, and carried into the building. For most of them, it was the first time they had ridden in a vehicle! There, they were fed first, and it was a treat to see that vast quantity of food disappear! Some ate with disbelief on their faces, like they had been half starved, and probably were!

Then it was time to be clothed, some for the first time in their life.

Used clothing of every description was tried on and viewed in a full length mirror. Some of them had never seen a mirror before, and were either enamored, or shocked with what they saw!

A moving picture of the life of Christ was shown with translation by Paul, and the gospel message made simple was clearly given to those who managed to stay awake on a full stomach! Then each of them received gifts of soap, a rolled bandage, hard candy, and a piece of raw meat to take home. It had been a full and happy day for them all, and they wore smiling faces back to their villages.

The following morning, an old man painfully hobbled up Chavuma hill and clapped at Wallace's office door. After their greeting, the old fellow poured out his complaint. "Yesterday was Cripples' Day. I heard the invitation, but I thought that you foreigners were going to kill all of us old, useless people, and throw our bodies into the river. But yesterday, I saw my friends come back to our village with full stomachs and fine gifts of clothing, shoes, meat, sweets, soap and bandages, so I have come today to receive my gifts."

With tender compassion, but to make an important point, Wallace responded, "I'm so sorry, but yesterday was Cripples' Day, not today."

"But sir, I didn't believe when I heard the invitation yesterday, but I believe now!"

Again, Wallace gently but firmly replied, "It's too late, yesterday was Cripples' Day" After the old man had gone, Wallace and Ruth prayed that he would make the crucial connection for things eternal.

Two days later, there was a clap [equivalent of a knock] at the door again. The same man appeared, and said, "Sir, I didn't believe when I heard the invitation to Cripples' Day, so I failed to receive those good gifts. I also once heard an invitation to come to Christ, to receive everlasting life, and I didn't believe. But I believe now, and have received God's gift of eternal life!"

This was exactly the lesson Wallace wanted the man to learn.

Procrastination in accepting Christ as Saviour could result in missing out entirely on God's free gift of eternal life.

Lesson learned, Wallace softened his approach and provided him with gifts as given to the others.

He returned home a changed man and rejoicing in the Lord.

"Behold, now is the accepted time; behold now is the day of salvation" (2 Cor. 6:2).

I'm Going to that Village

When we first knew him, he was a relatively young man. Sanjonji was an African Christian with a burning passion to tell others about the Lord Jesus Christ and about salvation through Him.

Wallace would meet him striding purposefully along on one of the many foot trails leading through the forests and across the plains.

Wallace would greet him, "Where are you going, Sanjonji?" With a smile the African would point in a given direction, "I'm going to that village to tell them about my Jesus." And off he would go.

Time went by, but Sanjonji would still be frequently found telling others about the love of the Lord Jesus Christ, or on his way to tell them. With stooped shoulders bearing the weight of increasing years, his footsteps would now be slower and more ponderous. "Where are you going, Sanjonji?" With the pointing finger, he would again respond, "I'm going to that village to tell them about my Jesus."

One day Wallace met him on a footpath. He was so stooped that he could barely raise his head to look forward. His swollen legs no longer moved by themselves. Sanjonji was using his hands to pull first one leg forward a few inches, then reaching for the other leg, he would pull it forward too. "Where are you going, Sanjonji?" The old man paused to raise his head as far as it would go. His wavering finger pointed ahead. "I'm going..., I'm going to that village to tell them about my Jesus."

Sanjonji took very conscientiously his Lord's requests, *"Go ye into all the world, and preach the gospel to every creature"* (Mark 16:15) and *"Be thou faithful unto death"* (Rev.2:10).

"He that Winneth Souls is Wise" (Prov. 11:30)

Wherever Ruth went she was always passing on a word for the Lord. She would speak to complete strangers telling them how God loved them so much He sent his Son to die for them so that they could one day be in heaven with Him. But she always reminded them that they needed to believe on Him and accept Him as their Saviour and Lord. Often when being entertained in a home by a Christian couple she would get talking to one of the children about their need to turn to the Lord for salvation. They couldn't depend on getting to heaven just because their parents belonged to the Lord.

Many people have told how they were led to the Lord through Ruth.

As an example, two of them are mentioned below.

Chavuma Mission had prayed about having a conference in 1937 and Wallace, along with a team of hard workers, had constructed a large building, which could seat 2000 people. This was called the 'Tabernacle' and was the largest single room building in Zambia at that time. Missionaries from the different stations and the believers from the surrounding areas were invited to join for a time of refreshing ministry.

While the men were fully involved with the preaching, Ruth, with all her work of preparing meals for the missionaries and their families who had come to the conference, was, as usual, looking for the ones and twos to whom she could pass on a word for her Master Whom she loved and wanted to share with others. She talked to Charlie Geddis, the 12-year-old son of Mr. and Mrs. James Geddis who were missionaries from Northern Ireland. They had been working in Angola and then came to work at Dipalata in Northern Rhodesia. Charlie listened as Ruth went over the story of Christ's love. He not only listened but that day he also trusted Christ as his personal Saviour.

Charlie grew up to be a real soul winner himself; leading many to the Saviour he had trusted as a result of Ruth's witnessing. He worked for many years in Northern Rhodesia (now called Zambia) as a missionary and is now enjoying the presence of his Lord in heaven.

Ruth Robinson, wife of Sam Robinson of Christian Missions in Many Lands in New Jersey, who along with her husband has faithfully served the Lord in the USA, tells how Ruth led her to the Lord when she was young.

Ruth would often say to ones she had been witnessing to, "Well I will be praying for you and when you come to accept

Christ as your Saviour, please write and let me know. I'll be looking forward to hearing your good news."

She not only reached out to others but also had the joy of leading some of her own children to Christ.

Grace, her youngest daughter tells about when the family was on furlough in the States, staying with Frances Tubbs, Ruth's sister, in a large double story house in Athens, New York. It was in the autumn but the snow had already fallen and Grace and her older sister Viola were playing together, going down the hill on the sled. They were enjoying it very much; such a change from Africa where they never saw snow.

Then the conversation changed and Viola started to tell Grace that Jesus was one day going to come back and take those who had trusted Him as Saviour to be with Him in heaven. This change in the conversation worried Grace, only five years old, as she knew she was not ready to go. If the Lord would come back for the rapture, since her parents and all her older sisters who had accepted Christ as Saviour, and her two younger brothers (who had not reached the age of accountability) would all go to heaven, she would be left behind alone.

She wanted to ask Jesus to forgive her sins but because her sisters had trusted Christ at the age of six she had got it into her head that you had to be six years old before you could do that. But Grace knew where to go. She ran into the house and found her mother who was busy packing because Ruth and Wallace were leaving the next day on a speaking engagement. Quickly Grace asked, "Mother, can I be saved today? I'm only five, not six, but I want to trust Jesus today. I want to be ready for heaven."

Ruth put aside her packing. "Why Grace, you are never too young to trust Christ," she told her, and went on to illustrate the Gospel by pointing to Grace's red dress with white cuffs – a picture of Jesus' blood which was shed on the cross to wash her sinful heart white as snow. She had the joy of leading her daughter to the Lord.

The family looked upon Ruth as a star who turned many to righteousness. As the verse says, *"And they that be wise shall shine as the brightness of the firmament: and they that turn many to righteousness as the stars forever and ever"* (Dan 12:3).

Welcome Travelers

The Logan family was back in the United States on furlough, visiting the Chicago area in 1953. They had been on radio at Moody Bible Institute, when Wallace received a phone call from Tommy Bartlett, the emcee of "Welcome Travelers" TV program. Could Wallace and the family come over to their studios right away? So the family got into the 9-passenger vehicle that had been wonderfully provided by the Lord for their use while on furlough.

Arriving at the studio they found people busy filling in forms and each member of the family was given a form to fill out, asking for details of places they had visited and what was their most exciting and thrilling experience. We all got busy writing about how Christ had come into our lives and saved us, when Tommy Bartlett came into the room and said, "Forget the papers, just come with me." He took us to his office and asked Wallace, "Mr. Logan, if I were to give you five minutes on our program what would you say?" Wallace told a few incidents of experiences in Central Africa. "Good" said Tommy. "Can you give us a ten minute program?"

Wallace said, "Well we would like to pray about it first." "Alright, go ahead and pray about it," said Tommy. While the family bowed in prayer and Wallace asked the Lord what He would have them do, Tommy remained in the room. As soon as Wallace had finished praying Tommy asked, "And what did God tell you?" Wallace agreed to give a ten-minute program.

When Tommy Bartlett returned he told us that he had managed to arrange for Wallace to have about 20 minutes. The family went on live and Wallace told of God's faithfulness down through the years in protecting them from harm and danger, providing for all the family's needs with not a cent promised by anyone. God had never let him down; the family had never had to go without a meal even though the nearest town was 500 miles away. Educational needs too had all been met. God was faithful.

The family then sang together, first in English:

"Away far beyond Jordan,
We'll meet in that land, oh! won't it be grand?

Away far beyond Jordan,
We'll meet in that beautiful land.
If you get there before I do
Look out for me I'm coming too.
Away far beyond Jordan,
We'll meet in that beautiful land."

Then in the Luvale language:

"Muze mu nganda yamwilu,
natuliwana ochokuwaha.
Muze musali yakufwa, natukaliwana cheka.
Kachi ove naulivangamo,
ngutalijize nangwiza nawa.
Haku mufwelela Mwata Yesu,
natukaliwana cheka."

After the program was over the family was treated to a delicious meal at a fancy hotel and also given a set of the *Encyclopedia Americana,* which proved to be very helpful when the children were studying by correspondence in Africa.

The family had been praying that the Lord would use the time on TV for God's honor and glory. Not long afterward, they heard that one young man had been watching the program and after seeing the family singing together, "We'll meet in that land, oh! Won't it be grand?" he switched off the TV and knelt down and trusted Christ as his Saviour. He had been the only one in his family who was not ready "to meet in that land."

"Ye shall be witnesses unto Me both in Jerusalem and in all Judea and in Samaria and unto the uttermost part of the earth" (Acts 1:9).

A Visit Inside the Arctic Circle

In the summer of 1965, Wallace and Ruth, had the opportunity to visit several assemblies in Alaska that had repeatedly asked them for a visit during furlough. They were accompanied by their daughter Grace and their daughter-in -law Ruth Ann. Their itinerary included a flight up to Nome and back. Arrangements were made for Wallace, Grace, and Ruth Ann to fly to Nome and back. Ruth stayed in Anchorage.

The morning of the flight, the three set out with exuberance to visit inside the Arctic Circle. It was indeed an interesting and fun trip.

When it was time for the return flight to Anchorage, the passengers boarded and were ready for take off. But they waited ...and waited ...and waited. Finally they were told that there was a mechanical problem with the plane and repairs would have to be made before they could safely fly. After further waiting aboard the plane, it was finally announced that the repairs were completed and they were ready to go!

Everyone breathed a sigh of relief when the plane took off skyward.

After about fifteen minutes of flying, over the intercom came the announcement that the plane still had problems, so they were turning around to return to Nome Airport. The passengers were somewhat anxious about this development, but the plane safely landed and the passengers were all escorted off the plane and into a nearby hotel lobby to keep comfortable while the repairs were done.

The stranded passengers were feeling quite nervous since their airplane was the only one at the airport and their only way out of Nome! Tension increased among them as they conversed about the malfunctioning aircraft. Finally, Wallace found the person in charge at the hotel and told him that he was a missionary from Africa and could tell a few African stories to help pass the time and get people's minds off the problems at the airport. The hotel officials gladly accepted his offer. After getting everyone's attention, they introduced him, and he got up to speak.

Wallace started telling stories of their experiences and the people's attention came to be clearly riveted on him. He told story after story of interest about Africa, acting many of the stories out, and was sure to include the spiritual application of each. After more than two hours of storytelling, he was still going strong when the word came that the aircraft was repaired and ready to go.

Passenger after passenger told of how his stories took their minds off of their concerns and worries about their current situation, and transported them overseas to the plains of Africa. Many thanked him for helping them calm down, appreciating his confidence in God, and not worrying so much about their trip back to Anchorage. A number of passengers commented to Grace and Ruth Ann that they were so lucky to have a Father like Wallace, who was such a wonderful comfort and storyteller.

The aircraft shortly took off and safely returned to the Anchorage Airport. That day, many lives had a taste of being inside the Arctic Circle, but came home more impressed with being in the interior of Africa!

"Preach the word; be instant in season, out of season." (2 Tim. 4:2).

"But sanctify the Lord God in your hearts: and be ready always to give an answer to every man that asketh you a reason of the hope that is in you with meekness and fear" (1 Pet. 3:15).

In Their Own Words

Letter of March 8, 1937

Ruth Logan wrote the following:

When we reached our first camping place, in visiting the villages, we heard the sad news that two men had been killed by lions. In the one case, the man had climbed the tree for wild honey to make beer, and did not see that a lion had stealthily approached the tree and was awaiting his descent. When he came down the lion killed him.

In one case when they were making honey beer a chief said, "Honey is for women, and beer for men." A Christian carrier said, "God gives us honey to enjoy, but don't let it make a fool of you by letting it ferment."

When we crossed a huge river full of crocodiles, we only had a stick with which to paddle. This broke in half in the middle of the current so we used our hands to paddle, praying that the crocodiles would not it bite them off, as they often do the tail of a fish. In fact yesterday we heard of a man who was grabbed out of a boat in the Zambezi River not far from here and all they found of him were his legs.

The second river we passed was named, *"Kwa kusavala vakwavo"* meaning "Let another sleep here." Naturally, Africans sleep near the rivers when traveling in order to have drinking water and water for food [fish]. As this river is not a very clean river, a traveler gave it this name many years ago. It is very mucky near the shores. We used the name of this river as a Gospel illustration. "Let another sleep here, not me." Those who want to follow sin and remain in the miry clay may do so; but *"As for me and my house, we will serve the Lord."*

Letter of April, 1953

Wallace Logan wrote the following on a ship board sailing back to Africa:

It is hard to express on paper our feelings and gratefulness to our Heavenly Father as we sit on the ship - our whole family sailing back to our loved work for God in Africa.

As the complete family pulled out of New York, how interesting to read the verse on the *Choice Gleanings Calendar* for that day, April 24, 1953, *"Thanks be unto God which always causes us to triumph in Christ."*

Mid-Ocean, April 26th: The sea is not rough nor is it calm. Some of us have our sea legs already, and others not yet.

On Sunday we were given an opportunity to have a meeting in the First Class Ball Room. It was a beautifully decorated place and passengers from all classes attended, and also officers and the ship's crew.

It was interesting the number that came to us after the meeting, speaking in a friendly way, and some bringing their spiritual burdens to us. One was heard to remark, "That was no modern sermon." Another said, "I have crossed the ocean over 20 times and been on many ships, and attended many services, but I never heard anything like that on a ship before. That message tells one plainly how to get to heaven."

The meeting led to another meeting in the theater, which they made available for this purpose, and we gave a talk on Africa, weaving in the Gospel. The family theme song seems to have spoken to many on the ship and we seek to continue to bear testimony to God's power to save whole families if they will let Him.

Bob [Young], Paul and David are sharing a cabin with another man who is an agnostic. It is interesting to hear something of their conversation, and I am sure the Scriptures quoted will give him something to think about. He said to them, "It is strange that I, an agnostic, should be put in with a group of Christians like you!" I doubt if he has ever had so many Scriptures to face before.

We continued our family Bible readings on this second ship [from England to South Africa]. This being a warmer trip, we can read on the deck. Several have asked to join us. We were having the morning reading on the deck and the evening reading in the cabin. The other day, some that attend the morning readings said, "We have been looking all over the ship for you in the evenings. Do you not have Bible readings in the evenings like the mornings?" We told them we do but hold them in the cabin, so now we have to have them also on the deck as our cabins are too small to hold them all.

The girls sat on the deck the other night and played a few hymns with their musical instruments, and soon a number gathered and joined in singing. This led to a few more coming to the Bible readings the next morning.

We asked for permission to hold a meeting and they granted same, giving us the use of the library lounge. They announced the meeting over the ship's radio. The lounge was packed and shortly after the meeting started, every window had people looking through into the lounge. At one window alone I counted 15 heads, filling one side to the other and up to the top. Many were standing on the decks within hearing distance. The captain came to Ruth and me a few days later and mentioned that several had spoken to him of how much they enjoyed it.

We were given an opportunity to speak to the crew and we felt the Holy Spirit speaking to hearts. During the meeting, which was held in the bowels of the ship, one of the crew stood at the door, inviting passers-by to come in and saying, "This is good. Come in or you will miss something." Some officers were present. One professed to be saved that night and several gave signs of the Holy Spirit working.

We felt the Holy Spirit working among the passengers, crew and officers. Four professed to be saved, so you folks who have been praying for us, God has heard your prayers -- pray on.

One night we had been up late talking to souls and it was

about midnight when I said "Good night" to one with whom I had been dealing.

Another man caught me by the shoulder as I stepped from the deck to go to bed. He said, "I have been following you for two days trying to get a chance to talk to you. Would you please spare a little time for me?" Praise God! It is not hard to lead a troubled soul to Christ.

He went away rejoicing after accepting Christ as his Saviour. Some of the crew asked if we could not go on to Durban in order to have some more meetings with them.

What a grand sight to behold Table Mountain again and be once more on African soil. We shall Lord willing start for the interior on June 23rd, and Lord willing reach Chavuma, August 6th.

Letter of November, 1961

Wallace Logan wrote the following:

The young missionaries have started a weekly village sing-song. They go to a different village each Thursday night and have community singing for about one hour. The villagers love it and during the week many come and ask when the sing-song can be held at their village. It gives great encouragement to see Africans, from time to time, remain behind and accept Christ as their Saviour.

It still sends chills up and down my spine every time I think of the poisonous spider, as big as a saucer, that jumped from the rafters of our house onto the back of my neck while we were eating our supper.

Surely the Lord protects in "slippery" places.

Letter of November 25, 1964

Wallace Logan wrote the following:

Ruth and I received an invitation from His Excellency the Governor and Lady Hone to meet Her Royal Highness Princess Royal at the celebration of the Independence of Zambia. Thinking we might get an opportunity for the Lord we accepted it.

Space will not permit me to tell much of the Lusaka celebrations but I want to say that God was honored, before 180,000 people, in prayer and Bible reading. The height of the excitement was at midnight when the Union Jack was lowered for the last time and the new Zambian flag was raised to the top of the pole.

The new President told how Britain had ruled well for 73 years, giving them a good foundation on which to build. "Guide me, O Thou great Jehovah" and Dr. Kaunda's favorite hymn, Psalm 23, were both sung and the the love chapter I Corinthians 13 and Joshua 1:1-9 were read.

Beer halls were closed for the day. I did not see one intoxicated person - white or black. The newspaper on the eve of Independence came out with large headlines "PRAY FOR ZAMBIA." We had the joy of speaking to many and giving out special tracts for the occasion. One professed faith in Jesus Christ.

Letter of December, 1966 - January, 1967

Wallace Logan wrote the following:

Christmas day was spent on the sea the day after we left Tamatave, Malagassy. The Captain asked me to have a service with the passengers, officers and crew. The Captain came to me afterwards to express his thanks and so did the others. We have had services every Sunday since embarking, and I must say it has been a very delightful voyage with many opportunities in visits with passengers, officers and crew alike.

Medical

Leper Island

Robin Island, a small island just off the coast of Southern Africa was at one time a sanitarium for people with leprosy; thus it was also reffered to as Leper Island. The chaplain of this colony invited Wallace to come and preach to the leprous patients there. He readily agreed and at the appointed time sat down on the platform observing the unfortunate people as they entered the church building.

The first arrival looked mighty good looking, as healthy as Wallace.

As they strode in and sat down in the auditorium, he thought, "I must have had a wrong impression about the seriousness of leprosy."

However, before too long the later arrivals had significant deformities. They were missing toes and fingers, some were blind needing to be led in. He realized that leprosy was indeed a serious disease which could result in marked deformity.

After the service the chaplain invited Wallace to visit leprous patients who were too sick or disabled to come to the meetings. One Christian man whom they visited was blind and severely crippled. There was but a hole making it difficult for him to speak and to be understood. The chaplain who could speak his language and understand him was able to converse with him. Above the head of his bed a text hung on the wall with these words. *"'Bless the LORD, O my soul, and forget not all His benefits'* —Psalm 103:2." "Does he know that Scripture text is there?" Wallace asked. The chaplain said, "I'll ask him," which he did. Back came the response, "He does indeed know it is there. Moreover he tells me it is his favorite verse!!" Wallace thought to himself, "Here is a deformed leper—without fingers, or toes, without lips, without eyesight and just a hole for his nose and this is his favorite verse!?" It seemed that the ailing man read Wallace's thoughts so he went on to explain, "I am thankful that I have no physical eyes to spoil my heavenly vision."

Wallace, in telling the incident said that he had been feeling low spiritually that day. The joy and faith in God of that Christian in the most tragic circumstances, uplifted him spiritually. Wallace was challenged to think that he had eyes, mouth, hands, and feet. Was he using them for the Lord?

"Bless the LORD, O my soul: and all that is within me, bless His holy name" (Ps. 103:1).

Groaning from Back Pain

Before going to Africa, both Wallace and Ruth had had some brief medical training. This came in useful, in situations where there was no other medical care available. The Africans eagerly accepted their help, feeling that any foreign medicine or medical care must be beneficial for general good health.

On one occasion a man, groaning loudly, cautiously moved into the room rubbing his back. They rubbed down his back with liniment, but the groaning continued, "OW..." They gave him aspirin, but the groaning persisted, "OW..." Local heat was applied. The groans kept coming.

When it was finally apparent that he was not going to get any more treatment, the groaning stopped and with his hands still on his back he said, "It's not me that hurts, it's my wife: she hurts here."

Occasionally, they would have the luxury of a visit from a doctor.

The complaint of one patient was, "I get back pain. It doesn't hurt when I work but when I sit for a long time, it hurts. If I sit only for a short time it doesn't hurt; I have to sit for a LONG time for my back to hurt." The doctor's response was predictable: "Don't sit so long. Next patient please."

Wallace would apply this to Christians, "Don't be sitting down on the job God has given us. Keep active for Him." *"Let us not be weary in well doing: for in due season we shall reap, if we faint not"* (Gal. 6:9).

Night Marauder

In a village hut a few girls were sound asleep. The usual night marauder stalked through the silent village. Stopping outside this hut, the heavy breathing of sleeping occupants incensed him to push aside the flimsy grass door.

The hyena grabbed the nearest head to the door, which was that of a young girl Pezo, and dragged her out of the hut. Still in deep sleep, she thought she was having a nightmare until the hyena put her down and started to chew away her face. Her screams aroused the villagers and the men came out with spears and knives. The treacherous animal unwillingly left his easy prey and escaped into the darkness of the bush.

Mangled Pezo with part of her face chewed away was quickly carried through the night to the mission station for medical help. As her wounds were being treated she was told of the One who was wounded for our transgressions and who willingly gave His life on the cross to redeem us. She gladly received the Lord Jesus Christ as her personal Saviour. The Lord granted healing to her bodily wounds but more than that, she was given her new life in the Lord. Pezo lived for many years with a very disfigured face - no lips to sheathe her exposed teeth—yet she joyfully said, "I thank the Lord for the attack of the hyena, for through that I have found true peace and joy in my Saviour."

After the hyena attacked Pezo, the people living in the village asked Wallace for the use of the trap he had for catching such rogue animals. Not many days after this a large crowd was seen ascending the hill to the mission station. Jubilant voices were heard singing songs of victory over their enemy that had been caught in the trap. The hyena, still alive, had been wrapped, trap and all, with a long sturdy rope to a pole that was carried by two men and brought for all to see. The crowd was increasing by the minute. One in the crowd was heard to say, "Look at the flitting and scared eyes of that hyena. It cannot look anyone in the face, because it has now been caught."

Wallace was never one to miss an opportunity to use for the Gospel. Here was a ready-made audience and this observation was just what was needed to bring home the truth of God's word, *"Be sure your sin will find you out"* (Num. 32:23) and *"the wages of sin is death."* Christ's great love in dying for our sins and our being justified by faith in Him was clearly proclaimed.

"Walk circumspectly, not as fools, but as wise ... redeeming the time, because the days are evil" (Eph. 5:15-16).

"That I might by all means save some. And this I do for the Gospel's sake" (1 Cor. 9:22-23).

Missionary Life

Israel—a Child's Impression

One time when Wallace and Ruth and their family were en route to Africa, a visit was made to the Holy Land. Frances and Esther, six year old twin girls, were given the privilege of being included with the adults visiting places of interest. This included the Western Wall, also known as the Wailing Wall, in Jerusalem. Eleanor, three years old, and Viola, younger still, were being taken care of by a babysitter.

When they returned from the tour, Frances and Esther rushed to see Eleanor and breathlessly asked, "Guess what? You know the Children of Israel? Well, they're all grown up now, and they're crying at the wall!"

Food Rationing in London in 1951

Wallace and Ruth with their seven children had traveled down the Zambezi River in a barge to Livingtone; boarded a train for a five-day trip to Cape Town, South Africa, and then embarked on a two-week voyage bringing them to Southampton in England. There they were able to visit with their sister in Christ, also a missionary to Africa, who was then residing in the UK.

The results of the Second World War were still very evident in Britain; food was short and people were still on food rationing. The first thing they had to do as a family was to go to the offices to procure ration cards. They filled up nine seats while waiting to be served. The lady behind the counter called to Frances who was seated nearest the counter to come up and be served, so Wallace jumped up with his brief case to go to the counter. But the lady turned to Wallace reprimanding him, "You go right back there and sit down, this woman was here first!"

"But we are all one family, Madam."

"Oh! Well come right on up then."

The lady wanted to give them ration tickets for sweets and chocolates but Wallace told her because they were on our way to America we would not take them but leave them for others there in England, who had been deprived of such treats during the war. That was fine and she appreciated the consideration. However when Wallace tried to increase the butter ration because "We are a big family of nine, Madam," her retort was, "That's not my fault!"

Later, their dear missionary sister had the whole family at her home for a special meal she had prepared – roast chicken, roast potatoes and vegetables they never saw in Central Africa. What a treat! The family was enjoying it to the full and Wallace started to offer seconds of roast chicken to her nephew who was seated next to him. As he encouraged the nephew to have some more, he also gave himself a few more morsels of chicken. The nephew quipped, "I'm glad I'm sitting next to you Mr. Logan!"

When the missionary sister, who recieved ration coupons for a single person, had no doubt had to save meat coupons for a long time to get enough saved to buy the chicken for this meal to serve eleven people. She then quipped, "Wallace, you don't need to finish up *all* the chicken in one meal!"

Humour

Status Symbols

In the early days, western apparel of any kind were rare among the Africans. Such things when acquired, were a significant status symbol. One Sunday morning the people had gathered in the Chapel and the service had started when a man walked in wearing a pair of shoes. His fashion statement and his pride of ownership did not go unnoticed by the congregation as he clopped down the aisle all the way to the front row. Taking a seat near an open window, he straightened his legs then conspicuously dropped his feet to the ground with a satisfying thump.

After the opening prayer who should come clip-clopping down the aisle but his wife—wearing the same pair of shoes! During the prayer, her husband had passed them out of the window to her so that they could get double credit for being the owners of a pair of shoes.

In Their Own Words

Letter of December 28, 1960

Wallace Logan wrote the following:

Someone gave us a Public Address System while home on furlough and Paul put it up on a 65 foot tower and then played carols. The people had never heard a voice from the sky before. Four people came running to us asking to be saved. The next morning the neighborhood people were all talking about it. One elder told how seven came asking to be saved.

Letter of May, 1964

Wallace Logan wrote the following:

Crossing the Zambezi in high flood is quite a problem. When crossing the river, it does not add to the pleasure of the trip to think back that every so often a dugout canoe has overturned in the swift current drowning the people. One day recently I was crossing the river going to my weekly Bible class with the assembly and to visit the villages, and the river seemed to be extra rough and the waves high. The waves were tossing the little dugout up and down when suddenly a high wave splashed over the boat drenching us all. The front paddler took fright where upon the back paddler, seeing the danger, shouted to him, "Drop to your knees and keep your head low in the bottom of the boat."

The boat was fast filling with water. I quickly removed all "ballast" from my pockets such as keys, handkerchief, purse [wallet], etc. and loosened my shoe laces. (I could have left my purse as it would not have caused me to sink!)

But I thought of that verse "Let us lay aside every weight." I did not want anything to hinder me from reaching the other side in case the boat did sink. It was not very comfortable sitting in two or three inches of water in the boat, hoping to reach the other bank before the incoming water won the day!! That day I had to preach with my back to the wall and back out of the hall by way of the back door.

When meeting anyone on the path I had to go into the bush and go around them!!

Army Ants (Letter of May, 1964)

Wallace Logan wrote the following:

I came to my office tonight to finish this letter. Suddenly I noticed army ants had surrounded the office. I am sitting with my feet up, hoping to finish this letter before they reach me. Ouch! there is one now! They are dropping from the ceiling by the hundreds into the southeast corner of the office. Soon they will force me out. Insects are running in all directions, some with army ants holding onto their legs and other parts of their bodies. It is interesting to see the spiders hanging calmly from their webs extended in the air. The clever creatures! Army ants will not attempt to walk on the spiders' webs. Evidently they are not tight-rope walkers especially on webs which are perpendicular! A centipede is rushing towards me trying to escape for its life. It is not welcomed by me for the two stingers on its tail are worse than the army ants' pincers! The ants are now covering the walls and floors and when I get down from my perch I shall have to make a quick exit. I'm glad I am not a centipede with all those legs for the ants to grab! They are getting too near me for comfort so "here goes!" I will leave the office to them till they wish to leave. Next morning, the army had gone, but not before finding a chicken which had roosted in a tree near the office and which the ants killed.

SHIKAHO!

A new missionary at Chavuma was learning the local Luvale language.

On one occasion after washing her dishes, she tossed the dishwater out through the kitchen window since there was no running water or drainage piping. This was her usual practice but on this occasion, to her horror heard a surprised yelp from outside—a man was passing by below the level of her window.

When she saw what she had done to the poor man, she rushed up to the next house where Wallace and Ruth lived. "How do you say 'I'm sorry' in Luvale?" she hastily asked. Ruth explained that to her knowledge, there was no such Luvale word as "sorry." "Perhaps you could say something like, 'I won't do it again.'" The new worker thought that this was woefully inadequate, so she rushed back to the hapless man and said what she thought was more appropriate, "Shikaho!," which loosely translated means, "Serves you right!"

Obedience to the Word: Spiritual Growth

"Owe No Man Anything"

A paid Christian employee of Chavuma Mission came to Wallace one day with a request: "Sakuunda, please give me a one shilling advance on my pay. I have already earned it so I would like the Mission to give me a shilling now and not wait for pay day at the end of the month."

Something about the urgency of his request prompted Wallace to ask why the employee was asking for the shilling ahead of time. "Well," said the man, "I was reading in my Bible last night by fire light and I read in Romans [13:8], *'Owe no man anything'*. I owe a shilling to someone, and I would like to pay him right away to obey the Scriptures."

"Be doers of the word, and not hearers only, deceiving yourselves. For if anyone is a hearer of the word and not a doer, he is like a man observing his natural face in a mirror; for he observes himself, goes away, and immediately forgets what kind of man he was. But he who looks into the perfect law of liberty and continues in it, and is not a forgetful hearer but a doer of the work, this one will be blessed in what he does" (Jas. 1:22-24).

Toloshi, the servant

Toloshi was a fine African Christian. A quiet man, he had a ready smile, a twinkle in his eyes and a fine head of white hair. He was of royal blood, and when the reigning chief died, Toloshi was next in line to assume the throne. Though urged to become the chief of his people in southern Angola, he declined. "I can better serve the Lord without that encumbrance" was his reasoning. (*"Wherefore seeing we also are compassed about with so great a cloud of witnesses, let us lay aside every weight...."* (Heb. 12:1)).

When Toloshi spoke, people listened. With a rich knowledge of the Scriptures he was a much sought after conference speaker in Central Africa. Not infrequently he would take odd jobs to help make ends meet for his family. He was an excellent carpenter and on one occasion when Wallace had hired him to do some work for the Chavuma Mission, he found him working hard, liberally adorned with sawdust and shavings.

Taking advantage of the opportunity Wallace asked him, "Toloshi, how do you explain that verse in 1 Corinthians 7:23, *'Ye are bought with a price; be not ye the servants of men?'* You're doing work for me. I'm paying you. So for now you are my servant."

Toloshi paused and laid down the hand-plane he had been using. "I think I can best explain it by telling you a story," he replied. "Years ago a large South African gold mining company needed workers for their mines. A representative from the mine came to our village and told the men about an opportunity to earn high wages. They would sign up for a year and would be paid very well for it. Many agreed to go and not long after, they were on a train bound for South Africa.

"After a month of work, they received their first payment. It was more money than they had ever earned before, but they were somewhat disappointed—somehow they had been led to believe that it would be significantly more. However, they stayed on to finish their year's contract; it still was good compensation.

"Sometime after they had returned home, an official from the mining company came to their village. He called for the men who had worked for his company. To each one he gave a large sum of money. They were astonished and bewildered. 'Don't you remember?' he said, 'That was the agreement. You were to get a small part of your wages in South Africa, but by far the biggest portion would be brought to you in your village.' The men, who had not understood the arrangement, were overjoyed.

"That's what I think that verse means," Toloshi continued, "*'Ye are bought with a price; be not ye the servants of men'.* Yes, I'm working for you, and you will pay me. But I'm really doing the work to please my real Boss in Heaven. By doing that, the superior pay by far, will be from Him." Toloshi picked up his plane and went back to work.

"Servants, obey in all things your masters according to the flesh; not with eyeservice, as menpleasers; but in singleness of heart, fearing God: And whatsoever ye do, do it heartily, as to the Lord, and not unto men; Knowing that of the Lord ye shall receive the reward of the inheritance: for ye serve the Lord Christ" (Col. 3:22-24).

In Their Own Words

Letter of February, 1961

Wallace Logan wrote the following:

Although we tried to make this follow-up trip a special visit to the Christians, it was interesting to see many who came and wanted to get saved. One old man in particular I noticed walking quietly at our side while we were walking from a three-hour meeting (they would not let us stop). As we walked, we talked with the Christians. After a while, the elderly man who was politely waiting until we stopped speaking, turned his head and quietly said, "I want to become a believer." We pointed him to the One who shed His precious blood on Calvary's cross and he accepted Christ as his personal Saviour. He is an eleventh-hour Christian. In some places we had as many as six meetings a day, starting at 6 a.m. and after the evening meeting some would come to our place and talk until midnight about the things of God.

Letter of December 21, 1960

Wallace Logan wrote the following:

At one place we were made happy by seeing the Prime Minister of the Luvale tribe going on well for the Lord. Three years ago we had a gospel campaign there at their capitol and he accepted the Lord as his Saviour. At that time he was given to heavy drinking and often encouraged to do so by European or white officials. When the District Commissioner heard that he had accepted Christ, he mockingly said, "I'll soon see if there is anything to his Christianity." So he invited him to a dinner with the express purpose of giving him plenty of liquor to drink. When the drinks were served the Prime Minister refused and said "I am now a Christian." The official seemed surprised and the next day remarked to another official, "Well, I believe the Prime Minister has become a Christian." When we were there this time the Paramount Chief of this tribe who is also a Christian told me the Prime Minister had not touched strong drink since the day he professed to be saved, and that he had led five people to the Lord.

God's Protection

Mbumbu and the Snake

"Would you go to my office where I keep my tools and bring back a screw driver," Wallace said to Mbumbu, his African helper. Taking the keys for the office which Wallace gave him, he disappeared.

Soon he was back without the screw driver, looking ashen—something major must have happened. He told Wallace this story. "When I went to your office I unlocked and opened the door. Immediately I felt moisture hit my bare chest. I knew exactly what it was so while looking down I covered my eyes with my arm and backed out the doorway.

"Then from a safe distance I squatted down, peered into the darkened room, and saw what I had suspected—a venomous spitting cobra in the rafters under the roof! You see, I am acquainted with these snakes, they not only have a fatal bite, but they can also spit blinding poison into your eyes. When you feel moisture hit you, you look up to see the source. Then the snake gives a full blast into your eyes. [The blindness is frequently permanent].

But I am aware of how they operate so I protected my eyes and backed out to some distance and said—'Woh, unapaye' [so there, I got the best of you!]"

Wallace thought, "How typical this is of Satan, our arch enemy, who uses the same tactics. When tempting us with what the evil world has to offer, he tries to attract our attention by some alluring aspect of sin, but does not show us the disastrous consequences of sin. It is only later that we find that there is a price to pay. The Scriptures tell us, *"When lust hath conceived, it bringeth forth sin: and sin, when it is finished, bringeth forth death"* (Jas. 1:15).

While on furlough Wallace would tell this story and apply

it spiritually. After returning to Africa he received a letter from a young lady in the States. It read, "Dear Mr. Logan, Thank you for telling the story of Mbumbu and the snake while you were visiting here at our Chapel. Before I was a Christian I would frequent dance halls reveling in the music and the immorality that often came with it.

"Yesterday, I was walking home from work and passed a store housing a dance hall on the second floor. The old familiar music caught my attention—and my interest. Before I knew it, I was walking up the stairway. The music got louder and I felt more attracted to it. At the top of the stairs as I was opening the door to enter, suddenly the story of Mbumbu and the snake came to mind and conscience. I slammed the door shut and re-treated down the stairs and ran home. I dropped to my knees and asked God's forgiveness. Thank you" she wrote, "for telling about Mbumbu and the snake."

"Goodbye, Sakuunda, Snake's Gone"

To his horror Wallace saw a good sized snake slip over the outside wall and enter the room where Ruth was bathing her baby twins.

Hurriedly she grabbed the two infants and took refuge in another room.

Concerned Africans kindly offered to find it in the house. In spite of all their careful searching, they found no trace of the snake.

As their helpers got weary, one by one they would say to Wallace, "Well, goodbye Sakuunda. I think the snake has gone now." Wallace and Ruth convinced themselves that the snake must indeed have gone outside unnoticed. So they called off the search, glad that the snake was no longer sharing their house!

Four days later a wise old African happened to come by and they told him about the snake that had entered their home, The African studied their faces then asked, "Did you see the snake go into the house like that?" As he said the last words he put a finger below each of his eyes and pulled the skin downwards, meaning "Did you really see it go in with your two eyes wide open? Or did you simply think you saw it go in?" Wallace assured him that it was the former. The African said, "Well if you saw the snake go in 'like that', then the snake is still in there because they prefer to stay in secluded dark places."

This unsettling news promptly led to a diligent search. Sure enough, they found the snake up in the rafters under the roof of their house (the house had no ceilings).

Since they had no desire to share their home with a highly venomous snake, they got rid of the intruder and thanked the Lord for the fulfillment of His promise: *"The beloved of the LORD shall dwell in safety by Him Who shelters him all the day long"* (Deut. 33:12). *"To whom ye forgive any thing, I forgive also: for if I forgave anything, to whom I forgave it, for your sakes forgave I it in the person of Christ; Lest Satan should get an advantage of us: for we are not ignorant of his devices"* (2 Cor. 2:10-11).

Whether the source of danger is physical or spiritual, knowing the habits of our enemy is crucial. Had Wallace and Ruth ignored the information the old African gave them, they would have put themselves at great risk from the poisonous serpent. To ignore the fact that being unforgiving puts ourselves at a great risk and at the mercy of that old serpent the Devil—who has no mercy—insures disaster of great magnitude. That can be readily avoided by obeying the wisdom of God's Word:

"Be ye kind one to another, tenderhearted, forgiving one another, even as God for Christ's sake hath forgiven you" (Eph. 4:32).

Crocodiles

Crocodiles in the Zambezi river took an annual toll of human life—Africans who had nowhere else to draw water for household use, to bathe, to wash clothes, or to fish for their supper. On one of their barge trips, Wallace and Ruth encountered a large crocodile which the local Africans, told them had been responsible for the loss of several villagers. At the request of those in the community, he shot and killed it.

"We were standing by this huge dead crocodile," Wallace related, "when suddenly it began to move. Jumping back, I took aim and killed it a second time. Glad to have it finally dead, we took several pictures with people next to it and some of our children sitting on it. All of a sudden it opened one eye! "Would you wait," Wallace would ask, "for it to open the other eye? No? Well we didn't either, so I grabbed the rifle and killed it the third time!"

It was common practice whenever a crocodile was killed, to open it up and see what there might be in it's stomach. Often interesting things would be found—sometimes sadly interesting things such as human remains. On one occasion, two bracelets, large and small, were found in the stomach of a crocodile, telling a silent and tragic story of the deaths of a mother and child ambushed by a crocodile.

On another occasion, Africans found an elongated object with a hard core and with apparent flesh around it. Thinking it was probably a human arm, the tissue was scraped off and to their astonishment they found it was the head and part of the shaft of a spear. This told the silent story of an African who had encountered the crocodile, speared it but did not kill it. The spear shaft had broken off and the wound healed. In subsequent years soft aggregate had accumulated around it.

In relating this, Wallace called to mind the spear that was thrust into the side of the Lord Jesus Christ as a final act of hatred of man against the innocent Lamb of God who had died for our sins. The Apostle John records this in the nineteenth chapter of his Gospel:

"One of the soldiers with a spear pierced his side, and forthwith came there out blood and water. And he that saw it bare record, and his record is true: and he knoweth that he saith true, that ye might believe." (vv. 34-35) The words of Christ are also recorded by John (5:24), *"Verily, verily, I say unto you, He that heareth my word, and believeth on him that sent me, hath everlasting life, and shall not come into condemnation; but is passed from death unto life."*

Leafy Bower

The first home that Wallace and Ruth had after getting married was a leafy bower. This was made from leafy branches of trees bent over to form a hut the shape of an igloo. This was a temporary home used while they constructed a more permanent residence.

One day news came that there was a man-eating lion in the area. Leafy bowers unfortunately had no protective door to close—just an open doorway. They asked the Lord to protect them then did what they could for defense. Using Wallace's own words in later telling the story:

"We tied a goat to a tree a short distance away, hoping that the lions had a taste for 'mutton' over man. Now I know what you're thinking, That's kind of hard on the goat, but if you had the choice between a lion eating a goat or you, I know what you would choose. Well we chose the same thing.

"We then piled pots, pans, and tin plates in the open doorway to give a noisy warning if an animal tried to enter. It would be awful to wake up and find yourself eaten, and not know what ate you! I laid a spear that I had at my bedside; my wife put a large butcher knife by hers. After again praying for protection, we went to sleep.

"In the middle of the night we were startled by the goat bleating vociferously. I grabbed the spear, jumped up, and tried parting the leaves to see what was going on. Meanwhile, my wife seized her butcher knife and, brandishing it in front of her closed ranks behind me. 'What do you see?' she asked excitedly wielding the large knife.

Trying to calm her I wasn't certain where my greater danger lay: before or behind me. I don't know if you've ever been in a predicament like that—a man-eating lion in front and an excited wife with a butcher knife behind you!

"Peering out between the leaves, I could see nothing in the darkness.

In time the goat settled down, and all was quiet in the dark African night, so did we.

"The next morning all was serene and the goat was intact. Later we heard that hyena tracts were found and presumed this was what was bothering the goat. We thanked the Lord for His protection." *God is our refuge and strength, a very present help in trouble* (Ps. 46:1).

Lightning Strike

Esther, 16 at the time, was in the washroom and used a large mirror over the wash basin while combing her hair. She had just walked out of the room when there was a colossal crash of thunder as lightning struck the house. The mirror she had just been using, exploded into innumerable shards of glass. Had she still been there, she very likely would have been blinded and her face severely disfigured. It could have taken her life. This was another example of the loving protection of a caring Heavenly Father, for which thanks was given.

It soon became apparent that the same bolt of lightning had set on fire the thatch roof of the nearby building that Wallace used for an office. It was "all hands on deck" to save the building with a bucket brigade. Thanks to the Lord the building was saved.

"Let all those rejoice who put their trust in You; Let them ever shout for joy, because You defend them; Let those also who love Your name Be joyful in You. or You, O LORD, will bless the righteous; With favor You will surround him as with a shield" (Ps. 5:11-12).

Poison Antidote

"Oh, NO!" The scream came from a mother who had just gone to check on her young daughter. Wallace and Ruth were guests in the home of their friends and fellow missionaries in Angola, at a remote mission station in central Africa. They had concluded a Bible study together and afterward their hosts' little daughter, Mary, had disappeared into another room. The alert mother felt that things were just a little too quiet, so she went to check. She was right; she came out holding an empty medicine bottle which had been kept in a high, inaccessible place Mary had gotten into. The nearest doctor was several weeks journey away. Grabbing a physician's family guide book they looked up the medication. What they found was terrifying: just a few pills could take a small child's life—Mary had consumed the entire contents of the bottle!

The book said that the best home antidote was to give the child the whites of eggs. There were no grocery stores, their food was bought from local Africans. Although eggs were available at certain times of the year, this was not one of those times. The two missionary couples knelt down and asked God to spare Mary's life and supply some eggs.

No sooner had they risen from their knees, than they heard a clap of hands at the front door—the equivalent in those days of a knock on the door. There stood a man holding one egg in the palm of his hand. They quickly paid him, took the egg, cracked it... and it was rotten.

At that moment, little Mary said, "Mommy, I want to go to sleep." The book advised, "Under no circumstances let the patient go to sleep: the child may never awaken."

"It seemed," said Wallace later, "that the heavens were made of steel, and only mocked our earnest prayer for deliverance." Once more they got on their knees and fervently asked God for the white of an egg to save Mary's life. Shortly, there was another clap at the door: it was an African with a basket containing a dozen fresh eggs. The egg-white was given to Mary and she was soon vomiting the pills and in time was her happy self again.

Mary grew up to be a dedicated missionary for the Lord Jesus Christ serving Him faithfully in Africa.

"Continue in prayer, and watch in the same with thanksgiving," (Col. 4:2).

I'm a Hunter

"Although quite short of stature, Maseka was a capable hunter. He told us about one of his experiences where he encountered a full grown lion only a short distance away. The lion apparently was after the same game (prey) that he was. Maseka knew that the worst thing to do would be to run—a moot point, however, since he was too tired from the hunt to even try. As their eyes met, Maseka wearily said to the lion, "You're a hunter. I'm a hunter. You go your way and I'll go my way."

Thankfully, the lion took Maseka's good suggestion and quietly left.

"When he came to the den ... The king spoke, 'Daniel, servant of

the living God, has your God, whom you serve continually, been able to deliver you from the lions?' 'My God sent His angel and shut the lions' mouths, so that they have not hurt me'" (Dan. 6:20-22).

On another occasion, Wallace was standing in a village conversing with Maseka. Suddenly a dog, made mad by rabies burst out of the forest howling fiercely. A bite would have been fatal. The dog was heading straight for them. Maseka had a sturdy cane in his hand and in the split second before the dog got to them, gave his cane a fast, hard circular motion connecting with the dog on its skull, knocking it senseless.

"The beloved of the LORD shall dwell in safety by Him Who shelters him all the day long," (Deut. 33:12).

Sapindalo's Bicycle Trip

Sapindalo was a fine African Christian and was an elder in the Chavuma assembly. Wallace and Ruth's youngest son, David, had the honor of being baptized by him. One of Sapindalo's brothers, Sakachama, was a converted witchdoctor who also lived a faithful and productive life for the Lord.

Sapindalo had occasion to go to Balovale 50 miles south of his home at Chavuma. For the pleasure of it, he decided to take along with him his young grandson who was delighted at the prospect. The next day he got out his bicycle and made his grandson comfortable on the seat he padded on the carrier. Off they rode.

After a while the little fellow patted his grandfather on the back and said, *"Kaka, nguli na lipwila"—* "Grandfather, I'm thirsty." He stopped the bike and got out an orange which he had brought for such an occasion. While peeling the orange suddenly a cold chill went down his back. There, not more than two or three pounces away, was a full grown lion sitting looking at him from the side of the road. The Lord gave Sapindalo the presence of mind to continue peeling the orange slowly as he prayed for protection. He said not a word to the grandchild: he knew that a sudden movement, or turning to flee, could provoke an attack. When they had finished eating the orange, he got on his bike calmly, (and possibly trying not to look delicious!).

The Lord continued to protect them and the lion never did attack. Presumably, the lion did not have a taste for a human meal with an orange side salad. Seriously, this is a modern day evidence that the God of Daniel is still strong to protect.

"The angel of the LORD encampeth round about them that fear Him, and delivereth them" (Ps. 34:7).

'Rap-Rap-Rap'

Wallace and Ruth were awakened one night by a strange sound: a soft, but rapid, 'rap, rap, rap' and then silence. This was repeated several times. Lighting the candle near their bed, they saw, to their horror, the reason for the sound. A poisonous snake was about to climb up the leg of the twin girls' cot but was stopped repeatedly by the lightning fast 'rap, rap, rap' of their cat's paw striking the snake's body.

Just as fast, the cat would leap away to avoid the lethal snake bite.

The danger of the situation was that if the snake had made it into the cot, an inadvertent movement of either baby could have drawn a fatal bite.

God used a house cat to distract and delay the snake's advance and allow Wallace time to get up and destroy the snake.

"He...that keepeth thee will not slumber," (Ps. 121:3). *"The LORD shall preserve thee from all evil"* (Ps. 121:7).

Army Ants

On another occasion, their baby in a cot near Wallace and Ruth's bed made a quick little cry which awoke them. Upon lighting a candle, to their amazement, the mosquito net covering the cot and the floor underneath the cot were covered with army ants, but not a single ant had penetrated the inside of the cot.

Army ants are killers, known to silently swarm over a victim and then they all bite together. Through this approach, the army ants have a time advantage for their attack. For younger or smaller victims, the result can be deadly.

In Their Own Words

Letter sometime during 1944

Wallace Logan wrote the following:

The other day just as I was approaching the house, my wife called out, "Just a minute! There is a snake at the door." Some Africans had seen it and ran to warn my wife. The snake was in the room between them and me, so I had to wait until they killed it before I could enter the house. It was a puff adder, a very poisonous snake. It is good to see the hand of the Lord watching over us daily. "God surely hears and answers prayer" as the hymn puts it, "and I know it full well."

Recently, my wife was sitting on the bed putting cool cloths on the head of our little David who was burning hot from a malarial fever.

Suddenly a tarantula fell from the roof on her arm. From her arm it dropped on the bed. There were exciting seconds that followed.

Ruth grabbed David while I tackled the tarantula. By this time it was in a fighting mood. I was empty handed, so it took some maneuvering. All had to be done as quietly as possible and not to excite David, lest his fever would go higher. Eventually we managed to kill it.

Yesterday I shot a huge snake in the kitchen. Now just as I am writing, there is a yell; and the children call to say a large snake just crossed at the front of our house. With snakes, tarantulas and scorpions often in our house and even under our beds; lions, leopards and a hundred other dangers on every side; one might stop and ask, "Why are we here? Why do we stay here?" The following will tell why.

A few weeks ago, one of our evangelists came and told how the assembly at the Kalasa out-station was full of joy over the salvation of a man and his wife, who have boldly come out for Christ, causing the whole country-side to marvel. Another evangelist, the same week, told of nineteen having trusted Christ elsewhere.

The Sunday before last, I was seeking to uplift Christ in a gospel meeting with over four hundred present. I told how

Christ bore the curse in Genesis. *"In the sweat of thy face shalt thou eat bread."* In the garden our Lord sweat as it were great drops of blood. *"Thorns and thistles also shall it bring forth to them."* We see the crown of thorns on His blessed brow, etc. One African stood up and said, "I can stand it no longer. You are right! I have sweat for my food and oh, the trouble I have had in sin! I want to come right now to the One you have told us about. I want Him for my Saviour."

Again, why are we here? Why do we stay? For over 20 years we have been kept from the many dangers so continue to pray and we shall continue to sow. Eternity will tell the results.

Letter of November, 1961

Wallace Logan wrote the following:

It still sends chills up and down my spine every time I think of the poisonous spider, as big as a saucer, that jumped from the rafters of our house onto the back of my neck while we were eating our supper.

Surely the Lord protects in "slippery" places.

Letter of December, 1966 - January, 1967

Wallace Logan wrote the following:

Left Durban, December 30, for Beira. Reaching there January 2, 1967 we anchored outside the dock for four days waiting for a working berth. From Beira on to Salisbury, Rhodesia where the saints showed us "no little kindness." While driving through the Zambezi Valley, suddenly about 200 feet in front of us three huge elephants crossed the road and looked at us. We drove on only to find ourselves in the midst of scores of other elephants, on all sides. We stopped to watch. They were throwing dust on themselves to cool off. They did not seem to be alarmed by our presence. So we stayed there taking pictures. A second car came along causing them a little more concern.

Finally when a third car arrived they showed their dislike by one of the bull elephants stamping its legs, flapping its ears and then charging. With that we all stepped on the gas and shot away. It was a relief to have an open road ahead of us. Pray on!

God is watching over us.

This letter has been written as we traveled along - bit by bit. I have had to cut down much of the detail for brevity's sake and even so it is long. I would love to mention names of many who have helped us along the way but if I did this would be too long a letter. Perhaps a book will be written one day in which some of these things can be mentioned. However it gives us much joy in knowing that a book in Heaven contains all such acts of kindness.

Letter of January, 1968

Wallace Logan wrote the following:

We have had our usual encounter with snakes, scorpions, tarantulas and other dangerous things but only to prove once again God's keeping power in answer your prayers for our safety. At one time we were having a snake experience almost daily. One day a spitting cobra passed within a few yards of where the children play. Then another day a python! The other day Lois noticed a large scorpion crawling toward baby Joy who was sitting on the floor and Joy is at the stage of picking up crawling things. So again we witnessed God's protecting power. Those who believe that God is dead had better not come to Africa! We are finding that not only is God living but He is a very present help in trouble and, *"Thou only makest me to dwell in safety."*

Everyday Events at Chavuma

Leopard's Stroll

Wallace and Ruth's home had a traditional African thatched roof. By 1946 termites had infested it and besides weakening it, it leaked when it rained. In addition, termites (locally called white ants) would fall from the roof in a very slow and gentle "rain" into the room below. To minimize the number of white ants on one's plate at supper time, one had to eat quickly.

Wallace planned to remedy the situation during the six-month dry season by replacing the roof. He also hoped to put on a more permanent, non-inflammable roof. After finding a temporary place for the family to stay, he remained on sight to do the necessary work. One full moonlight night he was standing in the roofless house silently looking at the beauty of the landscape before him, when a large adult leopard strolled nonchalantly on the road running in front of his home. The leopard stopped at a little water reservoir and leisurely lapped up what he wanted to slake his thirst. Satisfied, he continued his stroll and slowly disappeared out of sight. Either the leopard was not hungry or was upwind from a potential meal. But Wallace was thankful for the Lord's protection. It was exactly because of such an event as this that Wallace had sent away his family to safety.

The angel of the LORD encampeth round about them that fear him, and delivereth them. Psalm 34:7

Tidying up in the Bedroom

One morning Ruth was busy tidying up a few things in the bedroom before to going to the chores in the kitchen when she picked up Wallace's bathrobe lying on the large steamer trunk, which was used as an item of furniture for keeping linens etc.

As she did so she noticed what she thought was the belt for the bathrobe and reached over and down to pick it up. She suddenly dropped it and started crying out, "I had it in my hand. I had it in my hand." Wallace asked her "Had what in you hand, Ruth"? But the only response he got was "I had it in my hand. I had it in my hand". Ruth had not picked up Wallace's bathrobe belt, but a live snake! The Lord had once again shown His faithfulness and protection over His people – this time from what might have led to Ruth's death.

God's Provision

A Lion's Kill

Two African Christians who lived near Chavuma set out on a walking Gospel safari to tell in remote villages the Good News of God's salvation through Jesus Christ. They were obeying His command recorded in Matthew 28:19,20 *"Go ye into all the world and preach the Gospel."* While crossing a large grassy plain—a three day journey— they ran out of food. Knowing that God had promised to provide for them (*"My God shall supply all your need according to His riches in glory by Christ Jesus."* (Phil. 4:19)) they asked God to do so.

Confidently they continued across the plain. As they approached a small clump of trees, the sudden mighty ROAR of a lion stopped them in their tracks. A moment later a lion bounded out of the cluster of trees and ran, thankfully, away from them.

Curious, they went into the little island of trees and to their astonishment there was a fresh kill of an antelope. It is highly unusual for a lion to leave a fresh kill, unless forced to by a stronger power. For instance: a single lion will grudgingly abandon a kill when suddenly attacked by a large enough group of hyenas.

Though two men walking alone are no such force, there was a far greater Power that convinced the lion to leave its prey. They thanked the Lord for answering their prayer and enjoyed fresh meat for several meals while the rest of the meat was made into jerky.

The same God who provided food for Elijah through ravens (1 Kgs. 17:6), had provided for them as He will take care of all our needs according to His riches in glory (Phil 4:19) God supplies our needs *"according to HIS riches"*—that's a mighty big storehouse! And to accomplish His purposes, He will use anything from a bird to a brute beast.

"Casting all your care upon him; for he careth for you" (1 Pet. 5:7).

The Fuel Pump

The roads of Northern Rhodesia left much to be desired, but they did provide access to distant locations, and at the same time, a measure of adventure for those who wanted it or not. They featured a graded clearing and a few rickety bridges where necessary, and provided plenty of animal sightings, pot holes, and comfort stops along the way behind ant hills, some of which were thirty feet high or more. One of the worst of these roads was from Loloma Mission to Mwinilunga, where Sakeji School was located. This arduous trip was made twice a year in order to place the children of missionaries under the tutoring of devoted Christian teachers, who lovingly and gently opened their minds to reading, writing, and arithmetic, and God's claims on their young lives.

The Long Haul

This trip was planned and expedited by Wallace Logan in December of 1943, in his 1940 GMC pickup truck. He had built a mahogany rack over the truck bed on which to stack and lash down school trunks, spare tires, drinking water, cot beds, and anything else that might be required for the trip. It also provided shade for the passengers underneath. After traveling all day from Chavuma to Loloma Mission, where kind hospitality was offered and accepted, they struck out early the following morning with Mwinilunga in their sights, hoping to get there before nightfall. Shortly before noon, however, the faithful truck sputtered, coughed, and gave up the struggle. After a toolbox was extricated from the load, and proper analysis made, the accusing finger fell on the fuel pump.

The Bum Buy

In those days, smart people carried spare parts for their car, and Wallace was no exception. He had spare spark plugs, points and condenser, spring leaves, a fuel pump repair kit, and anything else that might be needed for emergency repairs. After disassembling the fuel pump, the repair kit was opened, and to the consternation of all, it was the wrong one! The diaphragm was too large, the linkage all wrong, and at this point, the otherwise happy trip went under a dark cloud. 1 Cor 10:13 came to mind. *"There hath no trial taken you but such as is common to man, but God is faithful, who will not suffer you to be tried above that ye are able; but will with the trial, also make a way of escape, that ye may be able to bear it."* Would this promise apply to this situation?

Relax and Trust

After laying the need before God, sticks were gathered for a fire, and water was boiled for the inevitable cup of tea, and the travelers relaxed in the shade of a Mukulu tree, waiting for the arrival of help from God.

Unexpected Visitor

The Mwinilunga shortcut, as it was called, was only traversed four or five times a year at the most, by missionaries or traders who swapped their wares for crocodile skins, animal hides, and such, and the probability was pretty slim that any would show up soon, or slimmer yet, that they would be in possession of a fuel pump repair kit for a 1940 GMC pickup truck! But God's power to provide cannot be underestimated! In a short period of time, a cloud of dust pushed another pickup truck into view, this time, a Ford. The driver was a well-known agnostic trader, who disliked missionaries, and their Lord, and often told them so. The Logans could have wished for anyone else in the world but him.

Tea Party

"Well, Mr. Logan, what are you doing up here in this forsaken neck of the woods, having a picnic?"

"No, we're having a cup of tea. Our fuel pump failed."

"Mr. Logan, don't tell me that you are stupid enough to travel these roads without a spare!"

"Oh, we have a repair kit, but they sold us the wrong one out there at Ndola."

"I'm surprised Mr. Logan. Surely you should know by now that you have to double-check everything you buy in this country! They will sell you anything to get your money! I can't tow you through all this sand, but I'll tell the government to send a truck out here to haul you in when I get to Mwinilunga."

"Don't you worry about us; we have asked God for the right repair kit, and it is on its way!"

With a sneer he climbed into his truck to drive on, but after a few meters, stopped, got his box of spares out, and came walking back with his fuel pump repair kit in his hand. "Maybe the diaphragm in my kit will fit your pump, Mr. Logan."

God's Answer

Well, it did! To his chagrin, the trader had bought the wrong kit for his Ford, but the right one for the GMC! After the pump was assembled and the engine running, he said, "I wish I had some of your Logan's Luck!"

"You don't need Logan's Luck, you need Logan's God!"

Then the full impact of it all hit him. God had used him, the agnostic missionary hater, to answer Mr. Logan's prayer!

He Is!

We don't know that the trader ever turned to the Lord, but we know that God, in His grace, gave him many proofs of His love and reality through contacts with missionaries in Northern Rhodesia. It is sad to see a man continue in his rebellion against God. This is blindness of the worst kind, and he will have no excuse when standing before the Great White Throne. Some day though, if he continued to reject Christ, he will know for sure, with eternal regret, that God is, and that He is a rewarder of them that diligently seek Him.

Roads

The roads of Northern Rhodesia left much to be desired, but they did provide access to distant locations, and at the same time, a measure of adventure for those who wanted it or not. They featured a graded clearing and a few rickety bridges where necessary, and provided plenty of animal sightings, pot holes, and comfort stops along the way behind ant hills, some of which were thirty feet high or more. One of the worst of these roads was from Loloma Mission to Mwinilunga, where Sakeji School was located. This arduous trip was made twice a year in order to place the children of missionaries under the tutoring of devoted Christian teachers, who lovingly and gently opened their minds to reading, writing, and arithmetic, and God's claims on their young lives.

Stranded in the Forest

Wallace, Ruth and their daughter Grace had been out to Lusaka the capital of Zambia on a business trip. They decided to return by a shorter but less frequented road. After spending the night at Luampa Mission station, they headed back to Chavuma. Before leaving the next morning they had contacted Chavuma by radio to tell them what time they were leaving and that they planned DV to travel all day and be home that evening.

The main road was passable although there were many potholes, but when they turned off on to the shortcut through the Black Forest, as it was called in those days, the road was a lot sandier and more difficult to negotiate. About halfway along they made a wrong turn and landed up in an area, where all the villages were enclosed with sturdy poles, showing the presence of wild animals in the area. Turning around they rejoined the main track through the forest but now the ruts in the heavy sand started to get deeper and they were really having difficulty making it in their two-wheel drive sedan, not made for such terrain! Then it happened! The vehicle got stuck with both back wheels digging deeper into the sand, until the chassis was resting on the road and the wheels just spinning. They could go no further.

They got out of the car and after working on the car without success, looked for shade to get out of the burning sun. Tying a mosquito net to a branch of a tree the three of them lay down on the ground with their heads and arms under the net to get away from the honey flies, which had started to buzz around their faces. If you squashed one fly the scent would attract many more till they would be flying into your eyes, nose, ears and mouth. The day wore on and not a sign of any other vehicle. They still had sandwiches, which they had for supper and then, to try and get away from the mosquitoes, which had now come out, they got into the car, where they spent an uncomfortable night sitting up – trying to sleep in between mosquito bites. They knew that a significant number of mosquitoes carried the deadly malaria parasite.

The sun rose the next morning and the day rapidly got hotter, bringing another more serious problem. Their drinking water supply was going down fast, so we rationed it out to only one small cup each, three times a day. Their minds started to think of stories they had read in Readers Digest and elsewhere of people being stranded in the desert and drinking water from the radiator to survive. Grace suggested that she start walking to get to the Watopa Pontoon on the Kabompo River to get help, but Wallace mentioned that often separating in a situation like that could bring worse problems. Also he said, "Remember the barricaded villages we saw just about 20 miles away. There could be many wild animals around here. Let's just stick together!"

That day went by slowly with the heat, honey flies, the rationing of water, and no proper shade all taking their toll especially on Wallace and Ruth. Right through the day, no vehicle came. In the late afternoon Wallace, the ever-cheerful but very practical one, said, "Well are we ready for another night of mosquitoes, sitting up in the car? What do you think Grace?" She replied "I think we'll be bouncing slowly along in the car singing choruses and hymns thanking the Lord for answered prayer, on our way to the pontoon." "Well, let's pray that you are right," replied her father.

Time for supper the second day! What could be done to lift the spirits a bit? Clear the bush in a different place and have supper there. So, they did that and Grace was planning on cooking some scrambled eggs, using an empty food can from a previous meal. That would be a change!

As she was getting ready they heard a faint noise as of a vehicle getting louder and then it stopped.

They listened intently and thought, "Oh No! The vehicle

probably turned off the road to go to that area of barricaded villages! If only we had put a sign on the tree at the crossroads to let anyone coming know that there was a car stranded on the road ahead." Their hopes, which had been raised, sank.

But no, again there was the sound of a vehicle! This time it got louder and louder until eventually they saw a large truck sailing along in the deep ruts, looking like a ship on the sea, coming toward them. It was a businessman from Kabompo loaded with his wares. He stopped and asked what the problem was. When he knew they wanted to be towed, he told them he would have to try to get around them without him getting bogged down in the sand.

As he was checking what he should do, there was another sound—this time from the direction of the Watopa pontoon. Within a few minutes a Land Rover appeared and in it were Christians friends of theirs from Balovale. Ronnie Drew jumped out and asked, "Can I help?"

"Do you have something to drink?" He ran to the car and brought back three bottles of Coca Cola. Up to that time they had always despised "warm" Cokes. But not that day! Were they ever welcome!

Ronnie got his vehicle turned around so that he could pull them out of their predicament. After he had done this, there was still the concern that their car could slip back into the ruts and would again get stuck.

Though it was dark by now, Ronnie very kindly went with them, stopping every few miles to check that all was going well. Two or three stops down the road they found elephant footprints. Another stop they found lion spoor right on the road, made since Ronnie had passed an hour or so before. They were all very thankful Grace had followed her father's good advice. And now on the way guess what they were doing?

Singing hymns and choruses, thanking the Lord for His goodness once again in meeting the need. At Watopa pontoon there was Paul, Wallace and Ruth's son who had come out looking for the lost party.

Elephant Meat—Answer to Prayer

The Zambian government enacted a law that the local fishermen could not sell their dried fish locally. It had to be sent to the cities where most of the people were. Consequently, we ran out of dried fish for the school girls [in the Chavuma Mission boarding school], and we were contemplating sending them home. When there was but one bundle of fish left in the warehouse, we held an emergency prayer meeting. Two days later, a message from the Angola border [6 miles north of Chavuma] came saying that one of the army lieutenants had shot a cow elephant, and would we be interested in buying smoked, dried meat for 2 pennies a pound! That was cheaper than the dried fish! The girls went crazy with excitement over the *"nyama ya Njamba"* [meat of an elephant], which, as everyone knows, makes one strong, and improves the memory!!

Several Land-Rover loads of bundled *"Njamba"* elephant were bought. We thanked God for His providing for our need in such a wonderful way and from an unexpected source.

Never one to miss an opportunity to apply a built-in object lesson, Wallace remarked "Missionaries need the hide and the heart of an elephant." That is, don't get offended easily and have a gigantic heart of love and compassion!

"My God shall supply all your need according to His riches in glory by Christ Jesus" (Phil. 4:19).

Got Any Rivers You Think Are Uncrossable?

It was time to take the twins, Frances and Esther, back to catch their plane at Balovale (now called Zambezi) for Livingstone. Then for them to travel five days by steam engine train to Cape Town, South Africa, to continue their studies for their Nursing and Midwifery Diplomas. Their suitcases were packed and piled into the vehicle for the 52-mile drive from Chavuma to the nearest airport. Wallace, Ruth, the twins and some of the children, got into the car and were off making good time. As they rounded a corner in the road, suddenly in front of them was the Makondo River, but there was no bridge in sight! The bridge was completely covered under fast flowing water caused by an unexpected flood in a very heavy down pour of rain in the rainy season. There was no way they could drive through such deep flowing water. Not only was it too deep but the river is noted for its heavy population of crocodiles! What could they do? No cell phones to call Balovale for someone to come from the other side to collect the twins, not enough time for a runner to go to ask for help and return before the plane would take off. The flooded river reminded the children of a chorus they had recently learned, so, turning to their heavenly Father who specializes in impossible situations, they sat on the banks of the flooded river and sang together:

"Got any rivers you think are uncrossable?
Got any mountains you can't tunnel through?
God specializes in things thought impossible:
He can do just what none other can do."

As they were singing they heard a rumbling sound and there on the opposite side of the river came a vehicle down to the river's edge. A friend of theirs got out of the car, waved to them, crossed in a canoe and came over to where they were. "Well hello! What are you doing here?" he asked. Wallace told him they were headed to the airport at Balovale to put the twins on the plane but they couldn't get any further because of the flooded Makondo river. Their friend then told them that he was on his way to Chavuma for a quick visit but had not heard about the bridge being flooded otherwise he would not have started out. How did the Lord make the uncrossable river crossable? They crossed the river in a canoe and took his car to Balovale in time to put the girls on the plane, while their friend took their vehicle and went on to Chavuma. By arrangement they met up again at the river the next day, switched back vehicles and returned to their respective homes. Do we have a God who can do what seems impossible and what no one else can do!

"Jesus said unto them, with men this is impossible: but with God all things are possible." Matt. 19:26.

In Their Own Words

Letter of July 30, 1936

Wallace Logan wrote the following:

We have just received word that a leopard has killed the cow of the African who was bringing milk to us. Milk is very scarce and we will miss it very much. The Africans do not mind it so much, for they always eat what is left of the kill and that is generally the whole animal less the insides. The wild animals after killing always eat the insides first and leave the rest until the next day. As a rule there is no next day, for the people claim it first! The Africans, also, when killing always eat the insides first, nothing goes to waste. A short time ago a man told me that he saw a dead animal on the plain. He went over and put his foot on it, and a lion jumped out of it. They were both so startled that neither knew what to do! The lion had killed it and ate the insides and then crawled inside and went to sleep. When the lion jumped out it stood looking at the man and the man at the lion. The lion then ran away. Later it returned and charged on him. The man was prepared and shot it. Surely this is a picture of Satan; he also hides in unexpected places, but by God's grace we can overcome him.

Salvation

Chief Sefu

Sefu, the Chief, lived at his capital some 20 miles west of Chavuma Mission. The following is an extract from a letter of Nov. 20, 1957 written by Wallace:

News has just come through of the death of Sefu, the Chief. Twenty four years ago, my wife and family, were with me in his capital. We had just finished preaching the gospel and at the end of the meeting, no one stirred. I then broke the silence by leaning over and saying to the Chief who was sitting next to me, "Chief Sefu, how about you and I going inside your enclosure (a six foot high grass fence giving privacy for the chief and his family) and you accepting Jesus Christ as your personal Saviour?" I shall never forget the words he said to me. They were these. "If I accept Jesus Christ on the inside of the enclosure will it not come out on the outside?" He then stood up and said, "Listen, my people, from tonight on your chief is a Christian."

He looked up to heaven and cried for forgiveness.

His public testimony did not please the headmen and the diviners and the heathen made a special effort to get him back. They called together out-standing diviners and they made a feast for the chief with the purpose of tripping him through heathen practices. As soon as the Christian chief realized what they were doing, he stood up and boldly said, "Goodbye." After a few days he started out on a trip to visit each village in his domain to tell them that he was now a follower of Jesus Christ.

The missionaries from Chavuma often visited him down through the years on their itinerating trips. He was taught the ABC's, given a few lessons in reading and from there went ahead and practically taught himself to read from the New Testament. You would see him early in the morning and many times during the day reading this Book. He was a succorer of many. During the past twenty four years he has lived to prove what real faith in the Lord Jesus Christ means and his fame as a Christian spread for hundreds of miles. Whenever you would use his name, both saved and heathen would all agree that he was a real Christian. For hundreds of miles both saved and heathen would confirm that he was a real Christian. He is now in glory but in his capital there is a little assembly that goes on for God and that will ever thank God for saving their chief from the darkness of heathendom.

(From a letter dated three days later) We have just returned from the funeral of the chief. He was buried in the bush a little way from his capital. A very large crowd gathered which gave a splendid opportunity to herald forth the Gospel story before those who gathered. Four expressed their desire to follow the Lord Jesus Christ. It was interesting to see heathendom and Christianity evident. Many Christians were gathered at the grave and the Gospel was preached. There were many dealing with souls at the grave and four came out for Christ. On the other hand the heathen practice is that no one that was present at the grave is to greet or contact the living chief, the successor, lest the spirits continue their work in killing more of the royal family. The procedure is that all that go to the grave side must stay in the bush and have a feast, generally they use cattle from the late chief's herd for the feast, and after eating they must curse the living chief. The spirits are supposed to be satisfied then that the living chief has enough enemies and trouble and they therefore do not kill him.

When we returned to the chief's capital, we found that the living chief was rather worried that we should come directly from the grave to him. And, of course, there was quite a large number of Christians with us who refused to go to the cursing party and came directly from the grave to the chief. We heard later that the chief said, "Well, because they are Christians it wouldn't do any harm!" So the heathen went to curse the chief and the Christians went to comfort him. The whole countryside will no doubt be watching to see what the results will be. In the meantime we are praying that the Lord will be glorified in it all that the heathen customs might be broken down.

"You are a people for God's own possession, so that you may proclaim the excellencies of Him who has called you out of darkness into His marvelous light" (1 Pet. 2:9).

No Hands to Thank God

An elderly woman came to Chavuma Mission for medical care. Coincidentally, it was noticed that she had no hands, just stumps.

Wallace and Ruth did not have the temerity to ask her why. It could have been a birth defect. Also, it was common in those days to punish a thief by cutting off his or her hands. Certain diseases such as leprosy could result in loss of fingers or even hands. They never found out the cause.

While at the Mission, she trusted the Lord Jesus Christ as her Saviour.

Her immediate joy was evidenced by a happy smile, but then her face clouded over. "I would like to thank the Lord Jesus for dying for me to take away my sin," she said. "But I have no hands." The way that the Luvale people said, "Thank you." was by clapping the hands. The word, *"Mwane"* often accompanied clapping the hands but was a generic term having multiple meanings. Again she repeated her dilemma: "How can I thank God without hands?"

Thoughtfully, she sat in silence then brightened. "Do you think," she asked, "Do you think if I strike these two stumps together that God will take that as a thank you?" Wallace replied, "I'm certain He would." She raised her eyes and the stumps of hands toward heaven then striking them together thanked God for the gift of His Son.

"Thanks be unto God for His unspeakable gift" (2 Cor. 9:15).

Age and Accountability

On a Gospel safari Wallace walked into a village and chatted with the villagers. Before he held an outdoor service he casually asked if there were any followers of God in that village. To his delight their response was affirmative--there was indeed. Wallace expressed his desire to meet him and off they went to bring him.

Before long back they came helping a very aged man to navigate toward Wallace. When they reached him, with great satisfaction they said, "Here he is: he is the Christian." "How do you know he is a Christian?" Wallace asked. "Of course he is a Christian," they responded, "He is too old to sin!" "But what about the sins of his youth?" to which they replied, "Do you mean those count too?"

The Psalmist David also longed for selective accountability when he yearningly wrote: *"Remember not the sins of my youth, nor my transgressions: according to thy mercy"* (Ps. 25:7). Unfortunately, however, all our sins count against us, permanently. 1 John 1:7 tells us how we can be forgiven for all our sins: *"The blood of Jesus Christ His Son cleanseth us from all sin." "Thou has set our iniquities before Thee, our secret sins in the light of thy countenance"* (Ps. 90:8). *"For our transgressions are multiplied before Thee, and our sins testify against us: for our transgressions are with us; and as for our iniquities, we know them"* (Isa. 59:12). *"For thou writest bitter things against me, and makest me to possess the iniquities of my youth"* (Job. 13:26).

Kambungo

"I'm due to speak at the meeting today," Wallace mentioned at the dinner table, "and I'm uncertain what to speak on." His oldest daughter Frances, always an idea person, responded, "Father, I have an outline that I've developed on the subject of the fallout from the curse due to the sin of man in the Garden of Eden. You are very welcome to use it if you want." Wallace looked it over and felt that the Lord would have him use it.

Included in the sermon, he read God's pronouncement to Adam from Genesis 3:17-19, *"Cursed is the ground for thy sake; in sorrow shalt thou eat of it all the days of thy life; thorns also and thistles shall it bring forth to thee; and thou shalt eat the herb of the field; in the sweat of thy face shalt thou eat bread, till thou return unto the ground; for out of it wast thou taken: for dust thou art, and unto dust shalt thou return."* Wallace went on to outline the gift of salvation through Christ to save us from the eternal curse of God because of our sins.

The sermon was interrupted by Kambungo, a man in the audience who had been listening intently. "What you say is true." He stood up. "I have labored in my garden to raise food for my family. I sweat and toil hard, but the thorns and weeds flourish all on their own. I know there is a God. When I walk through the forest I see plants and animals that only God, the Great Creator, could have made. I accept His Son to be my Saviour."

Kambungo (pronounced "Kahm-BOO-ngoh") was a changed man. His beaming smile left no doubt about who ruled his heart. Although he could not read or write he used the good memory that God had given him to tuck away significant portions of Scripture. He was present at every service, sitting in the front row with a happy look of eager anticipation on his face. When he preached, he did so with conviction, holding the open Bible (sometimes up-side-down) using as his text a portion from memorized Scripture. His knowledge of English was almost nil but he often used the one English term that he did know.

When he spoke to his Saviour in prayer he would frequently address Him as "Nahmbahlah Wahn" (Number One). He witnessed incessantly, telling others about his Lord. Regularly he would pick up Gospel tracts from the missionaries. He would then walk from village to village handing them out to people he met. God used him to bring precious souls to Christ.

Kambungo was not only a man with a message, but he also was a man with a mind and heart changed by God. He made his livelihood through his garden which because of his hard work was productive. Frequently he would sell his produce to the missionaries at Chavuma. On one occasion when doing so he said, "Oh by the way, this is the last of these vegetables for the season." "What do you mean Kambungo," he was asked, "the season is just starting? What happened?" Kambungo would not answer the question, but simply restated that the vegetables had come to an end.

Inquiry was made and the following story came to light. There was a headman of a nearby village who heard others giving good reports about Kamboungo's Christianity and was jealous. "Let's see what his Christianity is like when things aren't going well for him," he muttered. With that the headman got his herd of cows and drove them through Kambungo's prosperous garden destroying everything. When Kambungo was encouraged to seek redress, he would have nothing of it. He preferred to leave things in the hands of the Lord.

"Therefore, if anyone is in Christ, he is a new creation; old things have passed away; behold, all things have become new" (2 Cor. 5:17).

"He who looks into the perfect law of liberty and continues in it, and is not a forgetful hearer but a doer of the work, this one will be blessed in what he does" (Jas. 1:25).

Hat Near Bridge

While on furlough, Wallace and Ruth were traveling by car to a speaking engagement he had that evening. As they approached a bridge they noticed a woman's hat on the highway. They rounded the corner before the bridge and to their horror saw a woman climbing over the railing with the obvious intention of leaping to her death in the river far below. Pulling to a quick stop, Wallace jumped out and grabbed her before she could carry out her intention.

"Let me go, I want to die. Let me go," she cried hysterically as she struggled to break free.

"My friend," Wallace said gently, "what you need is a Friend."

"There are no friends in this world," she screamed, "Let me go, let me go, I want to die," as she continued to struggle.

"There is a True Friend who loves you. His name is Jesus."

Upon hearing the name "Jesus" she stopped struggling and quietly asked, "Do you think He could help me?"

His positive answer: "I know He can. Let's go to the car and talk about it." There, with Ruth praying silently, he led her to the Lord.

The three of them traveled on to the speaking engagement. Wallace and Ruth introduced her to the Christians there.

A few months later, Wallace and Ruth had occasion to re-visit that assembly which she had been attending. "Brother Logan," she commented, "what a difference between now and when you found me on the bridge."

"You were without Christ ... having no hope, and without God in the world: But now in Christ Jesus you who sometimes were far off are made nigh by the blood of Christ" (Eph. 2:12-13).

Family Altar

Each one of Wallace and Ruth's seven children recall with appreciation and pleasure the "Family Altar"—the daily gathering of the family to read a portion of Scripture together and have prayer.

Passages read were explained, often with an illustration, so that even the youngest could learn something. Questions would be asked.

Answers were sometimes humorous. Mark 2:3 reads: *"They come unto Him, bringing one sick of the palsy, which was borne of four."* The question was asked, "What does it mean, that the sick man *'was borne of four'*?" One hopeful response was, "He must have had four mothers!"

Additionally, each one in the family was expected to give a short thought on the verses read.

The Lord uses the daily family altar to convict a child, at an early age, regarding the need for a Saviour. The first four children trusted Christ at the age of six. When the fifth child, Grace, was under conviction of soul, she said to her mother, "I know I'm only five years old, but can I ask the Lord Jesus to save me?" She was assured that she could, and she did. The last two children also trusted the Lord as Saviour at five years of age.

The practice of having daily family devotions continued with each of their children in raising their families.

Testimony by Eleanor, third daughter of Wallace and Ruth:

"Some of my personal appreciations of Father and Mother were their putting God first in all things and their faithfulness in having family devotions with us every day. In the morning and in the evening the family was gathered for the reading of God's

Word. Difficult Bible portions which were read were explained and discussed so even the youngest could digest it. There were those inevitable questions that were asked at the end of the reading to see if we were listening and if we had grasped the truth of the passage. This continual intake of the Word was the means of my trusting the Lord as my Saviour when I was six years old and also helped me to grow in the Lord through His Word. How true it is that 'The Family Altar alters the family" and 'The family that prays together stays together.'"

David, the youngest, writes:

"I also have very positive memories of our daily devotional times as a family. They were interesting: an illustration or a short story to shed light on a passage of Scripture would often be used. The devotions were kept reasonably short. They helped me establish the habit of personal daily devotions. They taught me many excellent truths of Scriptures. God used them to convict me with my need of salvation, resulting in my trusting Christ at the age of five."

Daily devotions with the family are exceedingly important. Make them short, at least for small children. Make them positive and upbeat.

For small children, it develops more interest especially by acting out a scene from the Bible that you are reading. Encourage participation of family members by positive reinforcement.

In Their Own Words

Letter of November 30, 1945

Wallace Logan wrote the following:

One Sunday we had the joy of seeing a returned soldier break down and ask the Lord to forgive him. He said that he not only wanted to be saved, but also to give his life for the Lord. Very few connect the two together at the time of salvation.

We also had the joy of seeing a dear old woman (the mother of one of the Christian men in fellowship) come to Christ on Lord's Day. This is the third elderly woman saved within a few weeks. It is really lovely to see elderly, gray-haired people turn to God from their fetishes, after being bound with fear and superstition for so many years; now loosed and free, rejoicing in Him. Just after the meeting a middle-aged woman, who has heard the Gospel ever since the work at Chavuma began, came to the Lord. What a change there was in her face as Christ entered her heart.

Letter of February 8, 1968

Wallace Logan wrote the following:

The other day I heard the noise of a blind man's cane, tapping along the road. I looked out of the window and saw a blind man coming with his cane. When he reached our gate he, as though he had eyes, made a right angle turn. I went out to meet him., When he was within a few feet I greeted him and he stopped and said, "Are you Sakuunda (my African name)?" I replied, "Yes." He then said, "I have come to talk to you." I led him to a quiet place and we sat down. "I have come," he said, "and I want the Lord Jesus to forgive my sins and save me."

It was a joy to lead him to God's Son. After he was gone I got down on my knees and thanked God that the cane of a blind man could lead him to where I was in order for him to be saved. I prayed that I might be easily found even by people who cannot see they are in need of Jesus Christ. Now that same care is heard tapping down the aisle into the meeting.

Christian Challenge

"Casting Down Arguments" (2 Cor. 10:5)

While on one of his furloughs, Wallace showed his slides of the Lord's work in Africa at a particular assembly. One of the local Christians, who was also his host, was the projectionist. He did a nice job in changing the slides and it helped the presentation go very smoothly.

The next morning, his host asked him, "Where are you going from here, brother Logan?" Wallace gave him the name of another assembly in the same town. His host replied, "Surely, you're not going there, are you? I certainly wouldn't go there; our assembly differs from them on a point of doctrine and we have nothing to do with each other. In fact, I have a brother in the flesh in that assembly to whom I have not spoken in seven years."

Wallace replied, "I'm sorry to hear that—it was my hope to have you be the projectionist there also since you did such a nice job."

The reply was firm. "I can't go there!"

Wallace said, " Would you pray about it?"

"I'll pray about it, but I won't go!" Later that day, the host told him he would go on one condition. "Just as soon as the last slide is over," he said, "I want to slip out and leave."

"That's fine," was the reply.

That evening after the presentation, Wallace had for the moment forgotten the condition his host had laid down. He heard somewhat of a commotion at the back of the auditorium. The two brothers were hugging each other and weeping. They were heard saying, "Never again, my dear brother. By God's grace, never again!"

"That they all may be one; as Thou, Father, art in Me, and I in

Thee, that they also may be one in us: that the world may believe that Thou has sent Me," (John 17:21).

"You're Taking Your Daughters Back to Africa?!"

Wallace and Ruth with their seven children – five daughters in their late teens and twenties and two younger sons - were busy preparing for their return to Africa. The older girls Frances and Esther both nurses, and Eleanor and Viola both teachers had been praying much about returning to work as missionaries with the qualifications which the Lord had given them. They were now commended to the work at Chavuma in Northern Rhodesia.

While busy preparing to leave again for Africa they received a letter from one of Wallace's relatives saying, "Wallace you have no business taking your daughters back to Africa. How on earth will they find husbands in that far away country? Let them stay in the States where they can find suitable partners and settle down and have families. They'll be far happier here, than over there."

Wallace wrote back and told her that the girls had prayed much about it but each one individually believed God had called them to go back to help spread the Gospel through the vocations God had led them into. Two would return to help the many sick patients in the hospital while the other two would start a girls' boarding school. They would naturally all like to get married and have families but they knew that nothing was too hard for the Lord. He could provide even in Central Africa.

The whole family traveled back to Africa and got busy in their different activities. In time eligible young men started to visit Chavuma – some from Zimbabwe, Congo, South Africa and even the States - the Lord had started to provide partners for the daughters and wedding bells were then heard at Chavuma in Central Africa! And the partners joined in the work as missionaries too. It wasn't long before another letter came from Wallace's relative saying, "Dear Wallace, I see you are having a lot of success marrying off your daughters there. Can I send my daughter over to you to find a husband for her, because she is still not married?"

Truly nothing is too hard for the Lord! Each daughter was blessed with a husband who also was a missionary. Great is the Lord and greatly to be praised!

Providential Guidance

In 1941 World War II was raging. The Logan family, with seven children ranging in age from three to sixteen years old, was due to return to Africa by ship. Initially, the only booking available for them was on the *Henry S. Grove* a freighter which was laden with wartime equipment and ammunition. The passenger capacity was eight but the shipping line agreed to take the family of nine.

Shortly before the sailing date, nine berths became available on a passenger ship called the *Zamzam*. Repeated efforts to change the bookings to the *Zamzam* were turned down by Wallace and Ruth who felt that the Lord wanted them to take the first booking. The travel agent, Miss Wallace, although urged by others to make the change, followed Wallace and Ruth's wishes.

The freighter set sail on March 18, 1941, with the Logan family on board. Someone had told them that if the ship's engines stopped while at sea, it meant that there could be a marauding U-boat in the area.

War supplies on deck, although covered by tarpaulins, could have been clearly visible to enemy submarines. "I feel safe," the Captain said to Wallace, "with you on board." As it crossed the Atlantic, the freighter had three engine breakdowns but eventually made it safely to Cape Town.

A German U-boat mistook the outline of the Zamzam, and thought it was a warship. Full of passengers including other missionaries, the Zamzam was torpedoed and sank off the coast of South Africa. The Logans could have easily been among the victims.

Proverbs 21:31 says, *"The horse is prepared against the day of battle, but safety is of the Lord."* We should do all we can to prepare for upcoming responsibilities such as leading a Bible study, preparing for an exam, preparing for preaching or teaching the Word, and the like.

Leave the circumstances and the results to the Lord...He has all things in control.

Let us not doubt God's clear guidance even when circumstances develop which indicate a change should be made. We are told to keep our eyes on the Lord. *"I will guide thee with mine eye..."* (Ps. 32:8). *"Looking unto Jesus..."* (Heb. 12:2).

The Barge Captain

The beast of burden for the great water-ways of back country Africa was the river barge.

On one occasion, a missionary from another mission station had an important barge trip coming up, and because of the significant cost involved, gave some thought to ways of saving money.

He came up with an idea and shared it with his paddlers. "Most of you folks have been paddlers for years and I'm sure you know the river pretty well. A captain is paid twice the salary that you folks are. What do you say that we don't take a captain on this trip and I'll split half of his salary between you?"

The paddlers thought it was a great idea so on the appointed day, off they went without a captain. Things went pretty well until, toward the end of the day, they saw a large rock ahead. Some of the paddlers thought they should paddle swiftly to the right because, though narrower, the deeper channel looked to be there. Others thought if they paddled toward the left, there was a wider area through which they thought they could pass even though it was a shallower part of the river.

Soon, each paddler paddled in the direction he thought was right. All were paddling furiously! Everyone was yelling out their own instructions as to the direction they thought was best. Consequently, they traveled neither to the right nor to the left, but hit the rock instead. The barge high-centered on the rock and it started to tip to the right until all aboard thought they'd soon be dumped into the crocodile infested waters. Thankfully, it began to right itself , but then continued to tip to the left until they thought they would capsize to the left. Back and forth the barge rocked; no one had answers as to what to do now.

Though they were calling out and watching for help to come, no one responded. Night fell and the whole night was spent in rocking back and forth on the rock in the river.

At first light of dawn, there came a wave down the river that was a bit stronger than the current which thankfully lifted the barge off the rock and it slipped back into the river upright. The paddlers all agreed to paddle straight to the shore, and arrived without any loss of life or limb.

A man who knew this area of the river was hired to be the captain for the rest of the journey, and the missionary vowed never to start on a barge trip again without a captain. He never did.

"For it became him, for whom are all things, and by whom are all things, in bringing many sons unto glory, to make the captain of their salvation perfect through sufferings." Hebrews 2:10

Without a Captain in our lives, we will hit the rocks. We need a guide who is dependable and who knows the path of our river of life. *"The Lord shall guide thee continually..."* Isaiah 58:11

In Their Own Words

Letter of December, 1953

Wallace Logan wrote the following:

The other day while sitting in the meeting waiting for the hour to remember the Lord, my heart was lifted up in praise to God as I saw the Christians gathering and coming through pouring rain without raincoats, umbrellas or protection of any kind. I saw one woman walking through the rain with just a thin cotton dress and a baby tied on her back, both mother and babe drenched with the rain. In she came, sat down soaking wet and with the others that were also wet, from the rain quietly remembered her Lord. I could not help but think the love of God in their hearts would not permit the rain to hinder them from remembering Him.

Letter of March, 1955

Ruth Logan wrote the following:

We have just returned from the graveyard where we buried an outstanding Christian man. He was an ex-diviner and had married three wives. His fame as a diviner had spread far and wide but one day upon hearing the Gospel story he boldly came out for Jesus Christ. His testimony was so powerful that practically his whole village turned to Christ. His faith was spread abroad and people marveled at his testimony. He could hold people spell-bound for hours at a time. At one meeting in particular he held an audience of over 1,000 for more than 3 hours. No one moved – they sat with their eyes fixed on him, while he told how that Jesus Christ had freed him from the bondage of Satan and given him new life. He became known all over as a man of God and given to much hospitality.

I was asked to speak at his funeral. His younger brother also spoke and told something of what his life had meant to them in their village. He mentioned many things but these words stand out in my mind, "He has been a father and a help to us all." What a grand testimony. From sin's darkest pit – a diviner – to heaven's brightest glory with Christ. Thus we have witnessed the passing of a great man, picked by Jesus Christ our Lord from the heathen of dark Africa – does it pay to preach the Gospel?

Letter of January, 1962

Wallace Logan wrote the following:

Here in this part of Northern Rhodesia we thank God for the peace and quietness, also the friendly feeling in the neighborhood. Please continue to pray that we may use every opportunity for Christ and reach the unsaved while the door remains open. How long? The Lord only knows. But your prayers can help us reach many while it is called today. For the night cometh when no man can work.

We thank God to see every department of the work being used of God to win souls for Christ. The hospital, school, villaging work - building, repairs and all other phases.

Quite often Africans come for work to help us with our

building or repair work. They hear the Gospel, accept Christ and become spreaders of the Gospel in their home villages. When we are out in the distant villages we often come across them. It is also heartening to go to the Copperbelt and find many assemblies with Africans that were saved in this part of Africa now going on as starters and elders in these assemblies. We thank God for all who follow us in prayer. The rewarding day is coming! Pray on and share the blessing!

Letter of September, 1963

Wallace Logan wrote the following:

The great chief Mwanta Yamvu is dead. Hundreds of sub-chiefs of Congo, Angola and Rhodesia owed him allegiance. He was one of the most powerful chiefs in Africa. He had many wives. He had heard the Gospel from many missionaries and also from his wives. God works in wonderful ways. One by one his wives turned to God from idols. They started to tell the chief of their joy in Christ and besought him to become a Christian. At last he accepted Christ as his Saviour and by mutual agreement with his wives, he put down all but his first wife. [Editor's note: He saw the teaching of the Word of God, one man/one wife (plurality of wives was wrong). He arranged for the ongoing provision for those who would no longer live as his wives.] He boldly confessed Christ to all. When he visited us he spoke to the elders and to the Girls' School exhorting them to follow the Lord.

Shortly before he died he called his near relatives and said, "You have known me as the big chief, but I want to say that the only thing that is of any value to me now is my faith in Jesus Christ. I have no fear to die. I am ready to die." He then asked them all to follow God, work for Him and to be faithful to the Lord. Over 5,000 attended the funeral. Representatives from many countries including a representative of President Kennedy were at the funeral.

Letter of November 17, 1966

Ruth Logan wrote the following:

It was hard to hear a little two year old daughter say, "Daddy, I want to blow that too!" referring to the cigarette he was smoking. It reminds me of the verse in Ezekiel 16:44, *"As is the mother, so is her daughter."* The Africans have many wonderful proverbs. One is:

"Muzulu wa chombo natambula kuli Ise na Naye," which says, "The nose of the wild pig is taken after its father and mother." In short, our children take after the parents. How it behooves us as parents to live close to the Lord. "Draw me nearer, nearer blessed Lord." How I love that hymn Mr. Clapp often gave in the meeting, "Oh, to be like Him, we must abide near to our Saviour, close to His side...filled with His Spirit now and always."

Faith Tested

Samuel Logan's Death

The universal language of sorrow is understood by all people. A touching gesture showing kind empathy occurred at the funeral of their firstborn son, Samuel. An African woman, holding a baby of her own, said to Ruth, "Your arms are empty," and giving her infant to Ruth, offered, "Here, you hold my child for awhile." Ruth was deeply touched by the woman's thoughtfulness and accepted the kind overture.

Wallace had the difficult task of making his son's coffin and preaching the sermon at the funeral. God gave him the needed strength to do so.

"For this reason I bow my knees to the Father of our Lord Jesus Christ, from whom the whole family in heaven and earth is named, that He would grant you, according to the riches of His glory, to be strengthened with might through His Spirit in the inner man," (Eph. 3:14-16).

One day, young Frances asked her mother where her brother Samuel was buried. Ruth told her that she did not know, but she did know that he was in heaven. Matthew 19:14 says, *"Of such is the kingdom of heaven."* Second Samuel 12:23 says, *"But now he is dead, wherefore should I fast? Can I bring him back again? I shall go to him, but he shall not return to me."*

The way that Ruth accepted her beloved six month old Samuel's death, and her continuing concern for the lost spoke profoundly to the African women.

In Their Own Words

An Undated Letter

Ruth Logan wrote the following:

It surely has been a long time since writing to you but I have been laid aside for a while. The very night before I was ill the Lord gave me such a wonderful verse to cheer me and prepare me for that which was before me which was the theme of His power and His strength. No doubt the couple of shocks of Wallace dropping at my feet so seriously ill with malaria fever were not the best for me; he was so weak that we hardly knew what to do. In fact, I was alone on two occasions when he collapsed before me and he was too ill to leave for me to even call an African to help and while working over him, trying to bring him out of a dead faint, I kept praying, "Lord, if its your will you can send someone in the room to help me." And the dear Lord, so faithful and true sends in one of my children, little Grace. As she talks Lwena (the local language) as good as an African, I said, "Grace call Sapindalo" and she did. (Sapindalo is one of the Christians who I knew was at the other end of the house). He came and in short, the Lord wonderfully helped Wallace and he recovered.

While in Johannesburg where we had gone for a break, I had the worst attack of malaria I have ever had. Although, as I said a few times in the past, I thought Wallace was going home to glory and so did he think so, but God spared him. In this my attack of malaria fever the whole bed shook with the rigor and Wallace said he could almost feel the room shake from it. But oh, we have such a wonderful God who brought us both through these and now we are feeling better and hoping to see great things accomplished by the Lord in our lives. Yes, we'll praise Him for all that is past and trust Him for all that's to come.

Letter of February, 1942

Wallace Logan wrote the following:

A short time ago a neighbor woman was drawing water from the river when a large crocodile grabbed her. The next day part of her body was found on a nearby island. The next Sunday while in the villages telling the gospel story, we came across the poor husband going through the torture of their heathen ceremony. A dog was taken by the diviner, the throat slowly cut and blood taken while the dog died in agony. The blood was then mixed with medicine or concoctions of different kinds, which were put into pots of boiling water. Then this boiling hot mixture was sprinkled over the husband and relatives to keep the spirit of the dead away. You could see them squirm as the hot water touched their nude bodies. Thank God for Christ our Lord who has delivered us from such practices.

Letter of December, 1957

Wallace Logan wrote the following:

Recently we were called by one of the evangelists who wrote to say that a strong wind had blown the roof off of the meeting house and he, and several others, had been caught and pinned under the wreckage.

They had been pulled out and their lives spared. This damage came as a sad blow to us, for he is working in a district where there is much opposition from the enemy and we wondered how much the faith of the young Christians and the evangelist would be affected by this catastrophe.

Three of us missionaries and some of the local evangelists went with our vehicle to their place. When we reached them we found them full of the joy of the Lord, although there had been much damage done to the meeting place and some of them had kinked backs and twisted legs.

They told us it was the biggest windstorm they had ever seen and there were terrific torrents of rain. They had just finished a Gospel meeting and a large crowd had left the meeting house but the evangelists and a few others remained behind to shelter from the storm when suddenly the roof collapsed on them. Instead of weakening their faith it seemed to strengthen them and bring out the knowledge of the Scriptures. They rejoiced to think that God had counted them worthy to suffer as Job had suffered, when the wind blew off the roof of his house in which his children were gathered. They said, "They were all killed but we are all saved." They also mentioned that one catastrophe after another happened to Job but his faith faltered not.

One of them said, "It is nice to know that Job was a righteous man and God permits trials to come to righteous people to try their faith. It isn't that He doesn't love us that He permits strange things to happen to His children but He allows them that we might have a bigger reward in heaven."

I told them the story of the infidel in America who was a very prosperous man and owned several houses and everything was going well in his family. Then one day he accepted the Lord as His Saviour. He was a blacksmith by trade, and soon after his salvation things started to go wrong in his business. Then family troubles started. One day, one of his old infidel friends came to him and lost no time in making fun and jeering at his faith. The infidel said to him, "How is it that before you became a Christian you were prospering in your business and everything was going well in your home, but since you have become a Christian you have had family troubles and business troubles and everything seems to be going against you?" The Christian blacksmith said to the infidel, "Look here! you see this piece of steel?" and he took and put it in the fire and heated it till it was white with the tremendous heat. He then put it on to the anvil and pounded it with heavy blows. Putting it back into the fire and on to the anvil, he repeated this several times. After he had finished he had worked that piece of steel into a very valuable tool. Turning to the infidel he said, "You see this piece of steel. It has stood the test. It has permitted itself to be shaped, and is worth a great deal of money to me."

He then showed him a scrap pile. "These did not stand the test and they are valueless." Bowing is head he prayed, "Lord try me in every way possible but don't throw me on the scrap pile."

I wish you could have heard the prayers of those who went through this trial at this African assembly. They thanked the Lord for counting them worthy to go through this trial and asked that the Lord would strengthen their faith regardless of the circumstances of life. We have since heard that the villagers are marveling at their faith and they are having larger meetings than ever.

One thing rather touching was that the evangelist was building his house and was hoping to get it finished before the rains started. He had pulled down his old house in order to get the materials for the new one, but now he has stopped building his own house so as to put everything into the building of the new hall, while he and his family live through the wet season in a small shelter. Truly God has his jewels among these people. We shall appreciate your prayers that God will give many more in the little while that is left before He comes.

Prayer

Answered Prayer and His Care

Wallace and Ruth were living in a very crude pioneer dwelling. Expecting her first child, Ruth was supposed to have delivery at Kalene Mission Hospital, hundreds of miles away. But she went into early labor on Jan 16th. The only other missionary lady at Chavuma assisted her, the two working together without a doctor and with what knowledge they had acquired before coming to Africa.

A baby girl, Frances, was born without difficulty. Both the patient and the "obstetrician" breathed a sign of relief. But there was a surprise! Ruth's attendant exclaimed, "I don't think this is the only baby!" She was right! But there was concern because the next (and final) baby was a breech presentation. This represented a more complicated and hazardous delivery. Twenty minutes later the second twin, Esther, arrived safely through the goodness of the Lord.

Furthermore, the babes were not too premature to survive without an incubator.

A few months later (for it took that long for mail to reach them) a letter was received from a sister in the Lord in the USA which said, "Ruth, one night I couldn't sleep and I had a strong urge to pray for you. I got out of bed and kept praying for you ... Were you in any special need of prayer on Jan 16th?"

Praise God for His wonderful care and for diligent prayer partners.

Practical Praying

Ruth's prayers were very practical.

After the first four girls had been provided with partners,

Grace, the youngest, was still single. Of course much prayer was made that she too would be provided with the "right one" and at the "right time."

Ruth also believed that one's prayers should be practical and one should not expect God to do what one could do oneself. A young Britisher, David Croudace, had been commended to the work of the Lord from Rhodesia and had joined with John & Eleanor Sims in a new outreach at a place called Lukolwe on the west side of the Zambezi River. Wallace and Ruth had stayed a number of times in David's parents' home in Salisbury and Ruth strongly believed that their son would make an ideal partner for Grace. We will continue the story in David's words.

"John and I often drove back to Chavuma to collect things needed for the new work at Lukolwe. However, being on the west bank of the Zambezi we had to use a canoe to cross the river and then walk up to Chavuma in order to collect our goods. Usually when we arrived we would greet the folks and then go about loading everything needed onto a borrowed vehicle to take to the riverbank to be loaded onto the canoe. However Ruth would always give an invitation to us to have a late breakfast – John usually refused but I always accepted which suited Ruth fine. As I was about to enter their house I would see above the door, 'My Grace is sufficient for you!' Then Ruth would seat me at the table facing another text right in front of me, 'My Grace IS sufficient for you.'

"After enjoying Ruth's hospitality I would go out to help John with the loads. Whenever we visited Chavuma with the Sims family, knowing that I enjoyed my food, I was usually positioned next to Ruth at the table so she could ensure my plate was always full. At Christmas the Pile brothers from Cleveland would kindly send a very special and rich Christmas cake to the family. Ruth took charge of it and only one thin slice was allowed per person, in order to make it last. However when it came to me I was always allowed two slices!

"A short time later I felt led to move 50 miles away to Balovale (later called Zambezi) to work among the high school students at the large newly built government school. Every now and then when someone from Chavuma came to do business in the small township I would receive a delicious cake clearly marked 'anonymous – BUT please return the tin to Mrs. Logan.'"

Well the Lord answered prayer and wedding bells again rang at Chavuma when Grace, the last single one of the seven children, was married to David Croudace.

In Their Own Words

Letter written June 11, 1932

Ruth Logan wrote the following:

Here we are almost finished one week of the out-school drive.

Upon arriving we felt a real warmth in every Christian and our earnest prayer was, God keep us knit together with Him and with each other, for Satan will not be asleep, but will try in every way to bring in misunderstandings to hinder the work. Praise God in this, we haven't seen or heard of one argument, but rather a real burden for souls.

Every one every where, seemed to be on the alert to win souls. God is with us, for some who have held out against the Lord so long and were hard, said, "How can we refuse any longer?" At the out-school itself during the last five days, we have seen fourteen souls saved and the four at the hill the day we left. All you who are praying so faithfully answer the question – does it pay to pray?

Letter of November 1, 1937

Wallace Logan wrote the following:

(This letter is more meaningful since Paul, two years old, was their only son since the Lord had allowed the death of their first infant son, Samuel, ten years before.)

From Balovale we went to Chitokoloki, where Ruth and I and all the children felt the benefit of a week's change and rest. But I am sorry to say that Paul, who had been troubled with a little gland trouble (in the neck) became suddenly very ill. We traveled quickly to the government doctor at Balovale. The doctor examined him and told us that the child was seriously ill and he thought he would die. He diagnosed the case to be diphtheria, and having no antitoxin thought the case was hopeless.

He asked me if I was willing to have a plane bring up the antitoxin and, if so, we would try to send a wire from Mongu, which is 130 miles from Balovale. He said it almost seemed hopeless. Even by sending a special runner to wire to Livingstone from Mongu would take about six or seven days and he felt that the child could not live that long. We said we wanted to do all we could for the child's life, so asked him to send. The doctor said the only thing we could do until the antitoxin came was to pray.

Now our God often comes in on such occasions to prove His power, so we resorted to prayer. When the doctor came the next day he said, "I can hardly believe my eyes, such a wonderful improvement!" Well Paul maintained a steady progress and in three days time, we heard the sound of a plane, which flew over-head and brought the antitoxin.

This journey, two years ago, would have taken as long as three months, but by means of a special runner, who ran night and day to reach the telegraph office and a wire which was sent to civilization, a plane was here within three days, praise the Lord. The antitoxin was given, and Paul broke all records in steady improvement.

The doctor had given us permission to go back to our station. We were all ready to leave in two days' time for our recommended furlough when malaria made a wicked attack on Paul's heart. The doctor was called and he told us that it could easily be fatal and Paul had only one chance in a thousand of recovery. This again threw us back upon the Lord, and prayers for poor Paul have been going up from mission stations, missionaries and many for hundreds of miles in Central Africa.

Once again the doctor has expressed surprise in the wonderful improvement that Paul is making. This now is the twelfth day of Paul's steady improvement and we thank God for the gracious way in which He has helped Paul and us at this time. We are staying at the Rudges (Daisy' place) and they could not be kinder to us. Daisy is taking a shift in nursing Paul. The doctor says that if everything goes alright, we should be able to go back to Chavuma next Monday.

But, he said, Paul will need to be watched that he does not overdo for some time to come.

We have seen some wonderful answers to prayer since Paul's illness.

This one we would like to relate. Paul is very fond of orange juice and we thought if we could get some oranges, it may help him. Daisy had told us that there were no oranges at Balovale, so we asked the Lord if there might be some way or some place we could get oranges quickly. We could get oranges 100 miles north of Chavuma, but that would take two weeks to get them to us at Balovale, so we just prayed about it. In less than two hours an African came to the door with 15 nice big oranges. The doctor's wife wrote a note saying that these oranges had just come in from Mongu and she thought we would like them for Paul. We wrote telling her that God had used her to answer our prayers. Surely our God is wonderful. He hears and answers prayer.

Letter of March, 1962

Wallace Logan wrote the following:

We have been praying very much for the youths in our neighborhood. It would cheer your hearts if you could sit in our gospel meeting and see the large number of youths present. It is most encouraging to see several groups of a dozen or more at a time walk into the meeting.

Last Sunday after the service nine teenagers professed faith in Christ.

By your prayers and interest you become part of the work here, and you will one day rejoice in heaven to see people there praising God because you helped us to reach them with the Gospel Pray on and share the blessing. Never since the work began have your prayers for the work been more needed than at the present time.

Last Sunday Ruth and I went to spend the day with one of the African assemblies. They received us with great joy. One of the elders stood up and said, "We are very happy to have our spiritual father and mother with us today. Before he speaks to us I would like to say that they visited a village in our neighborhood about two months ago. After the meeting they spoke to a sick African. The missionary came to us elders and said, 'The man I have been speaking to is very close to becoming a Christian. He is not quite ready. I leave him in your care. Be sure to follow him!'" He then continued and said, "We want Sakuunda and his wife to know that we have kept our charge and the man is in the meeting today - saved and rejoicing in Christ." He then asked the man to stand up and give his testimony which he did.

After the service I went up and spoke to him. The man, Salwenyeka by name, said to me that he was rejoicing in sins forgiven and thanked me for visiting him in his sickness and leaving word for the elders to follow him. Nine others professed faith in Christ that Sunday morning too. So the blessing continues.

Pray on and share the blessing!

Letter of December, 1966 - January, 1967

Wallace Logan wrote the following on a board ship returning to Africa:

Visas: Thanks to God Who hears and answers prayer and to all you who were praying. Our final visas came just ten days before sailing. It looked very much at one time as if our sailing would have to be canceled. Not a very easy thing to do without a great loss of money, when everything was already at the dock or had been arranged to be sent to the ship. It finally sailed at 8 p.m. Saturday - 26 hours late. The sea was rough and it took us a day and a half to get our sea legs. The second night out, about 10 p.m. there was a sudden flash of light and then the whole ship was plunged into darkness. The engines went dead and the smell of smoke spread throughout the ship.

Some thought but did not dare say 'Fire.' We had to feel our way to our cabins - along long passages where stairways could have caused some nasty accidents with broken bones and necks. Some of the passengers called out, "I can't find my cabin." My brother-in-law, Bill Sacher, had given us a flashlight. We were able to help several find their cabins. It took them over an hour to get the lights fixed and over 2 1/2 hours to get the ship sailing. The next day the Captain told us of the great danger we had been in with our ship steaming full steam ahead before the blackout right into waters where other ships were and here our radar was completely off.

Letter of January, 1968

Wallace Logan wrote the following:

One of the highlights of the year was the Gospel Bus campaigns. Due to the pressure of the work we were not able to get started as early as we had hoped, but even though the rains had started we did not have to cancel one meeting because of rain. At one place, after having just set up for the evening meeting, the sky darkened with thunder and lightning crashing and flashing . I turned to an African Christian nearby and said, "It looks like rain." He replied, "O no, it won't rain for we Christians here asked the Lord to keep the rain away while the Gospel Bus campaign was on. It won't rain." And it didn't the whole time we were there. Suddenly a strong wind blew and cleared the sky of rain clouds. Sixty-seven trusted in the Lord there. The little assembly in this refugee camp was so cheered and encouraged.

They have since written to say that all were going on well and attending the assembly meetings and some were asking for baptism. Our main purpose was to visit areas where we have African assemblies and to encourage them in their most holy faith. God greatly honored and blessed. In all thousands of people were reached with the Gospel and many helped and encouraged. We thank all who have been praying for the Gospel Bus work and for the work of the Lord in general.

Tabernacle News

In Their Own Words

Letter of July 24, 1937

Ruth Logan wrote the following:

God has heard your prayers for our conference. Everyone spoke of it, as being one of the best conferences they have ever attended. It was inspiring to look on a sea of faces in the large tabernacle. Well over one thousand two hundred African Christians were gathered. The Breaking of Bread on Sunday morning was a sight to behold. In the Gospel meeting on Sunday, there were close to two thousand present.

Thirty three missionaries and seventeen of their children were present. Sixteen assemblies (not counting African assemblies on their own) were represented, from Congo, Angola, N. Rhodesia. S. Rhodesia, S. Africa and England. There were over twelve different nationalities and tribes; still by means of three languages all were able to hear.

We missionaries will not soon forget the special meetings held in our home and how God used our brother A.E. Rudge from England to feed us the Living Word. Also brother G.H. Mowat of S. Africa and brother E.H. Sims of S. Rhodesia gave us helpful ministry. Then the white children also had special meetings. God blessed this effort and one came out for Christ, while the others were edified and encouraged in the faith.

Although the meetings were intended for the edifying and building up of the Christians, still it pleased God to save some and restore others. It is hard to say how many were really reached, but thirty three are known to have expressed their desire to trust or come back to the Lord Jesus Christ. One chief and two prime ministers were among those who trusted.

A dear old African brother who was over eighty years old,

said to his brethren, "I will go to this conference and greet my brethren before I die." He traveled from a place eight days journey from Chavuma.

Everyone at the conference enjoyed his prayers so much. Three days after the conference ended he went home to Glory. He came into this part of Africa, many years ago, from northwest Africa as a Mohammedan, but when he heard of Christ, he chose the better and became a pillar in the church. Everyone loved him. He is now in the far better land.

The first Sunday of the conference we had the joy of baptizing 13 local Christians. The last Sunday, instead of having the afternoon ministry meeting in the tabernacle, the Christians divided into companies of about fifty and went into all the local villages preaching Christ. The neighborhood got a real stirring with the Gospel and much result followed.

On the last Saturday of the conference, the chiefs asked to have an interview with us. Imagine our joy when they said, "We have come to tell you that we are turning our country over to you for the Gospel."

Oh, what an open door! Dear ones, pray for us. Oh, that God would send forth laborers. Think of it! The country given to us for Christ. I ask, are not your prayers for us answered? Oh! continue to pray, as never before, and we shall see still greater things for our God; and you will one day rejoice with us. Praise the Lord for He is good! Pray! Pray! Pray!

We have just returned from exploring along a river about two days journey from here where we are hunting for a suitable site to open up another place for the Gospel. The Lord has helped us and, Lord willing, in the near future another Gospel center will be start in this spiritually dark land.

Letter of August, 1937

Ruth Logan wrote the following:

The wonderful conference we have so recently had was truly owned of God. The preparations for same required much forethought, careful planning, very busy days, weeks and months to successfully have such an occasion here in the heart of central Africa, especially being at Chavuma, which is away from the main lines or trains of any kind, where all communications had to be made by African carriers trekking over land, some by barge, two months journey to Livingstone (place of supply). But as we look back we simply say, How great is our God and oh, how faithful!

We had longed for a little foretaste of heaven in the having of this conference, by gathering together lonesome, isolated missionaries who were faithfully carrying on God's work with practically no fellowship of those of their own race, that the warm fellowship together would encourage and help them to go on with fresh strength for God. Then also the hundreds and hundreds of young African babes in Christ to be built up in their most holy faith through the ministry of the different missionaries and African brethren who have run well.

This we saw fulfilled and the slogan among the unsaved was, "These missionaries have a great God and He has a great crowd of His people following Him for we marveled to see how many were trusting in Christ."

The very atmosphere seemed so heavenly and no wonder to have had the privilege of having such pioneer workers who have gone through thick and thin for His name's sake and the Gospel's. One special request for prayer we had for this conference was that there would be no evil or unkind work spoken and this we saw literally fulfilled. We truly believe the Lord hearkened and heard not only in the ministry meetings as Christ was exalted and glorified, but also in the private conversations which always seemed upbuilding, and edifying a Godly concern one for the other, seeking to bear one another's burdens by prayer and loving Christlike interest in all.

Prayer was made some months before that we would not only be spiritually fed, but here in the wilderness as it were, He would provide a table – with no grocery shops around the corner or meat markets to ring up and give the order and as to vegetables, although we had ordered some seeds many months ahead to be planted, the locusts had so frequently affected our vegetable gardens, that we were cast on God alone for His help and wisdom. We were simply amazed at the way He provided. One very hot day I was wishing there was some fresh vegetable to put on the table. The morning meetings were finished, the other food was prepared and in ten minutes it was time for lunch.

As I walked out of the house to go to the small meeting house, which we had fixed for a dining room, for it was time to have the food put on the table, there passed a African with about three lovely heads of lettuce! How wonderful it seemed and it was on the table for lunch.

Letters of General Interest

Letter written sometime during the Second World War

Ruth Logan wrote the following:

The war has had its effect on the shortage of workers, so much so, as you have probably heard, we have been alone for a long time. Days are full-working, and growing-praise to God, many more saved and on their way to Glory through having taken Christ as their Saviour, thus removing fears and superstitions and giving them peace and joy instead. There has been so few letters come, that one does not seem to write, unless there is one to answer. Sometimes months have passed without hearing from home and loved ones, but we have so much to thank God for, all His great love, care and answering your prayers for us in His giving us strength for each day, as He always fulfills His promise.

Letter of April 1953

Wallace Logan wrote the following:

It is hard to express on paper our feelings and gratefulness to our Heavenly Father as we sit on the ship - our whole family sailing back to our loved work for God in Africa.

As the complete family pulled out of New York, how interesting to read the verse on the Choice Gleanings Calendar for that day, April 24, 1953, "Thanks be unto God which always causes us to triumph in Christ."

Mid-Ocean, April 26th: The sea is not rough nor is it calm. Some of us have our sea legs already, and others not yet.

On Sunday we were given an opportunity to have a meeting in the First Class Ball Room. It was a beautifully decorated place and passengers from all classes attended, and also officers and the ship's crew.

It was interesting the number that came to us after the meeting, speaking in a friendly way, and some bringing their spiritual burdens to us. One was heard to remark, "That was no modern sermon." Another said, "I have crossed the ocean over 20 times and been on many ships, and attended many services, but I never heard anything like that on a ship before. That message tells one plainly how to get to heaven."

The meeting led to another meeting in the theater, which they made available for this purpose, and we gave a talk on Africa, weaving in the Gospel. The family theme song seems to have spoken to many on the ship and we seek to continue to bear testimony to God's power to save whole families if they will let Him.

Bob [Young], Paul and David are sharing a cabin with another man who is an agnostic. It is interesting to hear something of their conversation, and I am sure the Scriptures quoted will give him something to think about. He said to them, "It is strange that I, an agnostic, should be put in with a group of Christians like you!" I doubt if he has ever had so many scriptures to face before.

We continued our family Bible readings on this second ship [from England to South Africa]. This being a warmer trip, we can read on the deck. Several have asked to join us. We were having the morning reading on the deck and the evening reading in the cabin. The other day, some that attend the morning readings said, "We have been looking all over the ship for you in the evenings. Do you not have Bible readings in the evenings like the mornings?" We told them we do but hold them in the cabin, so now we have to have them also on the deck as our cabins are too small to hold them all.

The girls sat on the deck the other night and played a few hymns with their musical instruments, and soon a number gathered and joined in singing. This led to a few more coming to the Bible readings the next morning.

We asked for permission to hold a meeting and they granted same, giving us the use of the library lounge. They announced the meeting over the ship's radio. The lounge was packed and shortly after the meeting started, every window had people looking through into the lounge. At one window alone I counted 15 heads, filling one side to the other and up to the top. Many were standing on the decks within hearing distance. The captain came to Ruth and me a few days later and mentioned that several had spoken to him of how much they enjoyed it.

We were given an opportunity to speak to the crew and we felt the Holy Spirit speaking to hearts. During the meeting, which was held in the bowels of the ship, one of the crew stood at the door, inviting passers-by to come in and saying, "This is good. Come in or you will miss something." Some officers were present. One professed to be saved that night and several gave signs of the Holy Spirit working.

WE felt the Holy Spirit working among the passengers, crew and officers. Four professed to be saved, so you folks who have been praying for us, God has heard your prayers -- pray on.

One night we had been up late talking to souls and it was about midnight when I said "Good night" to one with whom I had been dealing.

Another man caught me by the shoulder as I stepped from the deck to go to bed. He said, "I have been following you for two days trying to get a chance to talk to you. Would you please spare a little time for me?" Praise God! It is not hard to lead a troubled soul to Christ.

He went away rejoicing after accepting Christ as his Saviour. Some of the crew asked if we could not go on to Durban in order to have some more meetings with them.

What a grand sight to behold Table Mountain again and be once more on African soil. We shall Lord willing start for the interior on June 23rd, and Lord willing reach Chavuma, August 6th.

Letter of June, 1955

Wallace Logan wrote the following:

I seem to have developed a habit of waking up about three o'clock in the morning so I generally go around the house to see that everything is alright. Just the other morning I was making the rounds as usual.

I was not back in bed more than a few minutes, when suddenly I felt bites all over my body. Jumping up, I found that I was covered with army ants — and they were really working! By this time, several had their pincers closed into my flesh and others were just closing them.

This put me into a rather peculiar "jumping dance" while I slapped, plucked and pulled these off of my body.

After freeing myself, I rushed out with a light to see where I had come in contact with them and here I found that the kitchen, pantry and dining room were black with ants. They were marching off with insects of different kinds, including white ants, spiders, cockroaches, etc. The cat with two kittens had followed me out and suddenly they dashed back bumping into furniture as they fled in fear.

The dog outside must have been in for it as well for he gave a yelp and dashed away.

We had to vacate the kitchen end of the house and eat at John and Eleanor's place that day. By the next morning they had cleaned out everything that was of interest to them and marched victoriously on to their 'home' or camp. They made a good job of some of the insects that we had failed to kill with different poisons.

Letter of February 16, 1961

Ruth Logan wrote the following:

We had the Gospels translated into the Luvale language and they were working on the Epistles (Mr. Mowat translating in a mud building which is still here on the hill). We prayed that if it were the Lord's will we would have the whole New Testament in one book. How the Lord answers prayer, for we not only have the New Testament but the Old Testament too. The whole Bible hardly reached us before a religious group came in to try to keep the people from reading the Bible.

Letter of July, 1964

Wallace Logan wrote the following:

I am afraid that our worship meetings are not always as quiet as the worship meetings in the homeland. On this particular occasion two of Africa's most deadly snakes chose to drop from the branches above into the midst of hundreds gathered. The first one dropped about half way through the service causing the people to scatter in all directions.

They had no sooner gathered again when a second one dropped putting the people to flight once more. After the snakes were killed the meeting went on as usual! It is not uncommon for a couple of dogs to have a fight during the service or for a swarm of bees to fly through the audience. It was also distracting one day to have seven elephants pass within a stone's throw of the meeting place.

Some of these disturbances reminded me of a story I read which actually happened in England during the last World War. There was a shopkeeper and one night a bomb fell and tore off the front of the store. So the next day he put up a sign, "Open as usual for business!" That night another bomb fell and blew half the store apart. The next day he put up another sign "More open than usual for business!" The British nation has proven to the world that it can take it on the chin and so in Africa the meetings go on regardless of circumstances.

Letter of November 17, 1966

Ruth Logan wrote the following:

While we were on furlough in USA we had dinner with Mr. Kamuri Mbilishi, the Zambian Ambassador, in Washington, DC. He was converted in Zambia and is in fellowship at Washington. He had often spoken at Chavuma. He had to leave for New York City Sunday afternoon to welcome the President on Monday a.m. He asked Wallace, Ruth and Grace to come to New York City to hear the President's speech. Oh, the crowds of United Nations!! They look for peace and try to avoid war.

If only they would realize the One who can give peace is our Lord and Saviour Jesus Christ. Thank God for the two daughters of the Zambian Ambassador who accepted Christ Sunday afternoon before we left the home.

Letter of August 6, 1968

Wallace Logan wrote the following:

Our trip to town (over 1,000 miles return) for supplies, gave us much joy because of the contacts with many Africans and especially with African Christians and assemblies. One Sunday we visited the Charcoal Burners and found several from our part of the country, who were gathered in the bush to remember the Lord. Their meeting place was a cleared off area in the forest by the roadside. It was not a cathedral but had benches made of bamboo. They were made for worship and not for comfort! After sitting for two hours, when one stood up one could feel the corrugations on one's back and thighs. Where I sat there was a knob that projected right into my spinal column into the small of my back! The impression left was a continual reminder the rest of the day of the happy worship meeting with those African saints.

The pulpit was a pole stuck into the ground with a piece of box wood for a top. The table consisted of four sticks implanted firmly in the ground for legs and with bamboos tied together with bark rope for the top. They had found a piece of print cloth to cover the emblems for keeping off the flies. As we sat with them we could smell the "sweet" smell of charcoal. At the Breaking of Bread it was a joy to hear them pour out their hearts in worship, praise and thanksgiving to God for the death of His Son. After the worship service they insisted on both my son Paul and me giving a word of ministry. It was especially encouraging to know that the elders of that little flock were saved here at Chavuma and now had formed a bush assembly and that is only one of many such assemblies. We thank God for your prayers.

Chavuma 1923-1967

An Article by Wallace Logan that appeared in *Voices from the Vineyard* magazine. Fall 1967

"We are indebted to Wallace Logan and his family for this detailed account of the work begun by some of the Lord's dear servants (now in His presence), and now maintained by the Logans and their associates."

Chavuma is situated in the N.W. Province of Zambia, formerly known as Northern Rhodesia, and the Zambezi River, 6 miles south of the Portuguese Angola border. It lies approximately 12 degrees south of the Equator and 23 degrees east of Greenwich. The climate is fair generally speaking with warm days and cool nights. June and July are our cold season. 42 degrees is the coldest I have known it to get here and 120 degrees in the shade the hottest. We have two seasons a year—wet season and dry season which are pretty much the same in duration. The rains start in November and taper off in April with occasionally a few showers in October and May. The altitude is 3, 500'. Chavuma hill is 300' above the Zambezi River.

The Founding Work

Chavuma was officially opened in July 1923 by Mr. and Mrs. G.H. Mowat; Mr. and Mrs. E.H. Sims; Mr and Mrs. A. E. Horton and Mr. and Mrs. W.F. Logan. Mr. and Mrs. Mowat left in 1927 for South Africa because of the education of their children. During the four years the Mowats were at Chavuma they spent a great deal of time in translation work (of the scripture). They later returned to help out in the work on different occasions, at one time living at Lukolwe to help out the little outstation there. Mr. Mowat died on May 12, 1950 at Chavuma. Mrs. Mowat is living in South Africa. We thank God upon every remembrance of them and their great help.

Mr. and Mrs. E.H. Sims left for England in 1931 also for their children's education. Mr. Sims retuned periodically, making Chavuma his headquarters. During this time he made his famous donkey itinerary (using donkeys to carry the loads), when many people were saved in the distant villages. Mrs. Sims passed away in August and Mr. Sims passed into the presence of the Lord in January 1966 at Lukolwe. They served well in His work here. His son John married our daughter Eleanor on May 19, 1954. They both helped in the work at Chavuma until they with John's father left to work at Lukolwe in 1958 which was an outstation of Chavuma. Now a thriving work is carried on there by John and Eleanor Sims, Lorne and Betty-Lou Ferguson, David Croudace and Sandra Michie.

Mr. And Mrs. A.E. Horton left in 1924 to fill an urgent need in Angola, firstly at Kavungu for a short time and then to Loze and then back to Kavungu where they have labored ever since. The Hortons have been a great help to the Luvale field in the translation of the complete Bible plus the writing of a Luvale Grammar and Dictionary.

One thing that made a great impression on my mind that day we first arrived at Chavuma was the number of poles with skull bones on them, also the "mahamba" or fetishes in the villages we passed through as we walked from the barge at the river to the top of Chavuma Hill. The thought came to my mind, "Can these bones live?" Many a time we have knelt on the rocks of the hill and asked God to give us the people of this area for Christ. At that time there were very few villages but now it is one of the largest populated rural areas in Zambia. The people have moved n so fast and surrounded the hill that the Government has had to stop more from coming into the Chavuma area. The people were poor and wore mostly animal skins. They were not acquainted with money or its use and wanted cloth or salt instead. So many stretches of cloth or so many spoons of salt were used for payments of any kind. They lived in cone shaped grass huts with doorways so low that one had to crawl through them. Now they know the use of money very well indeed and they have houses which are greatly improved and wear clothes that many while people would covet.

The Arrival of Helpers

A few Christian came south from Kavungu and Kazombo in Angola, where the Mowats and Sims had previously worked for the Lord. These turned out to be a real blessing and help in the work here and became the first elders in the church and have been faithful down through the years. Some are still with us while others have gone to their reward in His presence. The great trials and persecutions which many of these and the first believers went through for their faith in God were the means of establishing a firm foundation in the work here. They were accused of being witches and wizards, were threatened with death, were told that the white people would eat their children. It went around that at the breaking of Bread we at the flesh and drank the blood of people we killed secretly. The early Christians had their homes burnt, fields robbed and attempts were made to poison them, etc. But through it all they came out strong unshakable Christians. One evangelist, Makina by name, was threatened in many ways. His mother, who lived near him was asleep one night in her grass hut when her grass door was tied and hut set alight. She felt the heat and tried to get out by without success—she perished in the flames.

Another evangelist and his wife were awakened one night by heat and smoke. They rushed to the door and found it tied. There was small window in their house, which very few homes had in those days. The destroyer had failed to notice this window and the evangelist and his wife escaped through it. It was too late to save anything and as a large crowd gathered, Sambaulu and his wife joined hands, while the flames were devouring his earthly goods and sang "We have a home eternal in Heaven." Today at their home village there is a large thriving assembly. Both he and his wife are outstanding shepherds of the flock.

Sanjonji was another of the many tried but faithful ones who was saved when he was about 50 years old through the early pioneers in Angola. He came down to help us in the new work at Chavuma. He was sorely persecuted with other when a certain chief went all out to destroy the Christians, threatening to kill them. God so helped the Christians to stand for Him that even the Chief became a Christian. I have made mention of Sanjonji often while on furlough, telling how he wore out his legs going to the villages to tell about "his Jesus." When his legs gave in he used a cane and when he could no longer use a cane, he took his hands and shoved his legs to the villages, in order to tell others of Jesus. I was called one day to his village. I crawled into his hut where he was on his death bed. He looked up at me and said, "Sakuunda (my African name), these legs of mine will take me to no more villages. I cannot even get up and shove them. I have called you to ask if you will continue to use your legs to go and tell my people about my Jesus." I said "Yes Sanjonji, I shall, and not only my legs will be used but also those of my wife and seven children. We shall all continue to tell your people about your Jesus." I wish you could have seen the joyful expression his face as he closed his eyes and entered into the presence of the One he loved and served so faithfully.

Chavuma Hill was chosen for health reasons. In those early days we were still losing missionaries from Malaria and Black Water Fever. We did not have the wonder drugs which we today have for Malaria. So we chose a high site to get away from the mosquito breeding swamps. The Barotse were then ruling and had the land rights. King Yeta, a descendant of King Liwanyika of the Barotse, refused to grant the site. The government officials encouraged us to stay on. We could not find out why the Chief was refusing the hill site. He was very friendly and told us that we could have any other site we wanted, but not he hill. We prayed on! Then one day the mystery was solved. Shortly after we had arrived on the hill we started to dig a well at the base of a large anthill. We had been told that water could be found under anthills. After digging very deep we found no water so gave us the hunt. The ant hill earth was left piled up next to the hole. We discovered one day that a rumor had gone around that we had been digging for diamonds—the chief had wanted the hill if there were diamonds and therefore had refused the site. We then wrote and told the chief that we were not digging for diamonds but digging a well trying to find water. We told him that we were not interested in diamonds or the riches of this world but had come for the souls of the people—to make known our Lord and Saviour to them. We told him that the hill site had been chosen because of health reasons only. The site was immediately granted. We were after "diamonds"—not the ones men search for—but "black diamond's," praise God, and we have found them! Hundreds, yea thousands—"jewels for His crown."

When we started to develop the place we put in wide roads, not that we expected to see a vehicle here, for 600 miles of forest and bush lay between us and the nearest place of civilization, but we thought that roads were better than narrow bush trails. It is easier to spot sakes and animals on a wide road. Where one road joined another we put in a culvert. Fifty miles away from Chavuma is a Government post. From there, the people were taxed about 50 cents a year as an attempt to make them feel a responsibility toward good citizenship. But the Africans, like a good many others, never entered into the real value of taxes! So the majority became tax defaulters. After the roads were made and large culverts put in, quite often Africans would come to me and say, "Thank you for putting in the nice culverts. Before they were in we had to flee the bush to hide when a tax collector came, now we just hide in the culvert and he walks right over us and we come out after he is gone." We were then able to tell them of a better hiding place in Christ from the coming judgment.

Although at the present time Chavuma is manned by American missionaries, in its history we have been blessed with very godly co-workers from other countries including England, Scotland, Australia, Canada, South Africa and Rhodesia. Others of special mention here are the following:—Miss Gladys Richards (now retired); Miss Doris Mitchell (who married Mr. Deubler of Chitokoloki); Miss Daisy Wareham (who joined the Deublers of Chitokoloki); Miss G. Erma Motter (now Mrs. R. Criswell); Mr. And Mrs. Fred Barnett (both now in Glory); Mr. And Mrs Geo. Butcher; Mr. And Mrs. Mike Howell (now serving the Lord at the Zambia Christian Press in Ndola). We are also grateful for the help that Linda Frown (now Mrs. Wm. Walden) gave in the hospital at the a time when we were very shorthanded; also for Miss Jeanie Young's valuable year of service in time of need.

The present workers are:- Mr. And Mrs. Wallace Logan; Ben and Frances Iler (at present on furlough); Bob and Viola Young; Grace Logan; Alice White; Paul and Lois Logan; and Joyce Finch. Frances, Lois and Joyce are nurses and Viola, Grace and Alice are teachers. All those sisters, apart from their professional duties are very actively engaged in S.S. classes, women's work, village visitation, etc. The men, apart from their general missionary activities, are kept more than busy with building, maintenance and general upkeep of the station. We are so glad that the Lord has sent practical minded missionaries to Chavuma — willing to do anything necessary to keep things going. For missionary work does not mean sitting under a palm tree teaching one's Bible.

In closing this article the following incident comes to mind. While itinerating in the early part of the work, we camped in a certain village. The head man of the village stood up while the meeting was still and professed and said he would like to trust the Lord Jesus Christ as Saviour. After a minute we invited him to our tent to help him in the step he had just taken. As he left to go I said, "I will walk with you to your house. "With that two or three Africans who were with me also came along. They went inside his house while I stayed outside and after saying "goodbye" we started back to camp. On the way they turned to me and said "He will never stand O! He'll never stand." "Why not?" I inquired. "O! the idols and fetishes in his place are everywhere. On the bed. In the bed, under the bed. The walls are covered with them. We have had fetishes and worshipped them but we have never seen anyone with so many. O! He'll never stand." I replied, "Now you must no limit the Holy One of Israel. That was one of the worst sins that Israel committed. You must pray for him and God is able to make him stand."

Many years later we were out in a different direction itinerating and far from this headman's village, when we came across and little group of Christians breaking bread. There I recognized the headman who had accepted Christ despite his house full of fetishes. He told me this story. He said that a few years after he trusted the Lord he left his village and had come to visit his relatives. They were all fetish worshippers. "I told them of the better things I have found in Christ," he continued, "many have accepted Christ as their Saviour. Some have learned to read and we are remembering the Lord who died for us."

How we thank God for the many co-workers in the home-land who have been behind the Lord's work at Chavuma in more ways than one. We look forward with joy to the coming day when we shall hear Him say to them, "Well invested, good and faithful servants!"

Looking Back

As They Got Older

As they got older, Wallace and Ruth tired more easily and being in need of a break for refreshment and renewal had agreed to go to South Africa for that break. They flew from Zambezi to the Copperbelt and were staying with Mike and Esther Howell in Ndola while waiting for their visas to be granted.

During that time of waiting, Wallace had a stroke. In the next several days, his overall condition deteriorated, and it appeared that he had a heart attack. He was taken home to heaven on February 5, 1969. (More details of this are found in *A Man Called Sakuunda*, in the first section of this book.)

In Their Own Words

Letter of February 12, 1969

Excerpts of a letter written by Bob and Viola Young:

Father's home going was on February 5, 1969. On Sunday February 9, the funeral was held at Chavuma at the foot of the hill, with 700 to 800 attending from various parts of the country. Catholic priests, Hindus, army officers, and government officials were there to hear the Gospel powerfully preached.

Another message was given at the funeral by a faithful African elder who dearly loved Father and always considered Father his best friend on earth. In his message he said, "Another man of God has been taken from our midst to spend eternity with his Lord. May the Lord grant each one of us that remains the wisdom and grace to carry on for His glory."

Father is now enjoying a well earned rest in the presence of his Lord, Whom he served so faithfully for 46 years as a missionary. His joy is now complete and he has received His, "Well done, good and faithful servant."

It is heart-warming to hear hundreds of voices triumphantly sing, "He doeth all things well."

Since Father's home call several in the neighborhood have been saved and others have dedicated their lives to Christ. May the blessing continue.

Of Wallace It Was Said

Of Wallace it was said...
"We saw Christ in him."
"He lived what he preached."
"He lived up to his African name, *Sakuunda*, 'Father of Peace'."
"He had a tremendous capacity to forgive."
"..was slow to speak, quick to hear..."
"He suffered for Christ."
"He was a true shepherd to us all."
"He loved God's Word."
"He was easy to be entreated." John 3:17
"He had a great burden for the lost."
"I was never in his presence but that his conversation turned to Christ."

He often said...
"Take God at His Word."
"Have you ever said to the Lord, 'I love you'?"
"Live your life so that you will have no regrets."
"Don't let the lack of fellowship [with another believer] be on your part."
"We are not living for time, but for eternity."
"Let's tell the Lord about it."
"Be a man for God."
"Make sure you have a family altar."
"Always speak well of Christ."

Further details of his home going are given in the first section of this book, *A Man called Sakuunda*.

In Their Own Words

Letter of March 20, 1969

In a letter dated March 20, 1969, Ruth wrote to her brother and sister-in-law:

Six weeks ago yesterday Wallace went to live with Christ in our heavenly home, where we will soon meet with "the Shout." Oh do pray, Fred and Louise, that I may be found faithful. How glad Wallace must have been to see his Lord he lived for and served. Wallace frequently spoke of meeting the Lord without any regret. Yes, he did live for the Lord and to die was his gain. We can never thank Him enough for His great faithfulness and just when we need Him the most, He is the nearest. There are three words which are among my favorites – CHRIST IS ALL. He's the Lily of the Valley, the Bright and Morning Star.

One has to be up early to see the morning star and it will be only the Christians who will see the Lord when we meet Him in the air, whether living Christians or those asleep in Jesus. What a blessed hope is ours.

From a letter written July 21, 1971 Regarding Ruth's home call:

Letter from Grace Logan, Bob and Viola Young, Mike and Esther Howell, and Paul and Lois Logan, all the Logan "children" who were at Chavuma on July 19, 1971.

Dear Ones In Christ,

On [Monday] July 19, 1971, Mother passed peacefully into the presence of her Lord. Exactly seven months before, she had suffered a slight stroke which caused facial paralysis from which she recovered. A serious circulation blockage developed later causing gangrene in her right leg. After much prayer Dr. Worsfold of Chitokoloki Mission scheduled an amputation here at Chavuma for June 5, and she "came through with flying colors." She was very keen to get an artificial leg and we had high hopes that one day she would be up and about again. But the

Lord had other plans for her. Mother went down quickly at the end after several heart attacks.

On the Saturday morning before Mother passed away, Mike came in to help take her out for her daily ride; he sank into the wheelchair while waiting for us to get her ready. Mother turned to us and said, "Come on, Esther and Grace, let's take Mike out for a ride in the wheelchair!" She enjoyed that last ride into the sunshine after which she had a visit with an African elder, encouraging him as he faced an important decision. Sunday morning she asked about going to the meetings. She longed to be with the Christians again but was too weak. [On Monday morning] Mother had slipped away to be with the Lord. Congestive heart failure had taken her.

The funeral was held at 11 a.m. Tuesday. There were about 900 present, with folk from different areas. Included in the number were missionaries, government officials, chiefs, heads of schools, their staff and pupils, two Ph.D students and a priest (from a nearby Catholic mission) to whom Mother had witnessed at Father's funeral.

Mr. James Caldwell spoke in English, commenting, "Ruth Logan was a devoted wife, a loving mother and an ardent personal evangelist." He told how she would be by her husband's side out in the villages, taking the children with her. Charlie Geddis, another missionary, gave a word of testimony at the grave side. He thanked the Lord for having brought Mrs. Logan into his life for when just a boy he had been led to Christ by her. Our Head Teacher also, an elder in the assembly here, spoke in Luvale telling how when he had applied for work in 1931, "Nyakuunda" first took him aside to tell him about the Lord. He added "No one could stay in her presence long without hearing about her Saviour."

An answer to prayer was the triumphant note at the funeral. Some of the Africans were discussing why the losing of a loved one could be faced with such fortitude and some suggested, "It's because they are educated, that's why." But the Christians disagreed, saying, "No, it's not education, but Christ."

News of Mother's home-call has reached the towns and villages bringing a real sense of loss to many who knew and loved

Mother. Typical of letters of condolence received from Africans was: "We have missed a keen and hard worker of our Lord Jesus Christ in Chavuma as well as the whole province. She was one of the best and faithful present day disciples of our Lord serving God in the world in bringing people to Christ. She was also one who helped many married and unmarried, old and young women in Chavuma to love God and their husbands. Therefore brothers and sisters may God comfort you all and let's look forward to the day when we shall meet them in our heavenly home. Let's read together John 11:25-27."

Mother's life was characterized by zeal and she did nothing halfheartedly. Whether cooking or baking for a conference of 50 missionaries or praying for her husband as he spoke, she did it heartily, as to the Lord. On many occasions, we remember, her meal untouched, she would gladly spend time with the bereaved or leading a soul to Christ.

Philippians 1:20-21 were two of her favorite verses. Just as in her life God used Mother to the salvation of souls, so also in her death over 70 trusted Christ.

She faithfully prayed for each member of her family.

Mother's interest in souls was keen to the end. Paul had planned special English meetings to reach the teachers in the area. For five consecutive nights between 25 and 30 teachers attended. When told about these meetings, though very weak, Mother asked, "Is there anything I can do to cooperate?"

Characterizing her Christian testimony was her desire to "strive together for the faith of the Gospel," an example for us all to follow.

O Mother Mine

The floor was mud, the roof was grass,
No silver, gold or chrome:
The walls were made of sticks and stones,
Yet Mother made it home.

She carried us when we were babes
And taught us how to pray;

She washed our faces, combed our hair
And told us to obey.

She soothed our brows when we were sick;
Surprised us with a toy,
And though she loved her family
The Lord was her chief joy.

She loved the souls of those around
The ones by sin enslaved,
In earnestness she plead and prayed:
"If only they were saved."

She loved to sing: "I'm Thine, O Lord,
I've heard Thy voice to me."
But now she sings a grander song
With Heaven's harmony.

For angels came and carried her
To be with Christ up there
At home with Him and all His own,
A place beyond compare.

Just like the stars she shines above
She won lost souls below.
O Mother mine, how very wise
You've used your time here so.

Written by Frances Ruth Logan Iler

Looking Ahead

Closing Remarks

The family sang many, many times together with others:

"Away far beyond Jordan, we'll meet in that land, oh! won't it be grand?
Away far beyond Jordan, we'll meet in that beautiful land.
If you get there before I do look out for me I'm coming too.
Away far beyond Jordan, we'll meet in that beautiful land."

These two committed and humble servants of the Lord, Wallace and Ruth, are at home in Glory. They were ordinary people who committed themselves to the God and Father of our Lord Jesus Christ, who gave Himself to win forgiveness of sins and reconciliation with the Father for lost mankind. They gave themselves for Him to use however He wished. They loved their Saviour and desired to live their lives for His glory; their passion was to bring lost souls to the Lord Jesus Christ so that they also could receive His wonderful salvation.

In Their Own Words

Letter of February, 1961

Wallace Logan wrote the following:

The time is short. Let us be soul-conscious. It is an awful thing for a soul to perish when Christ has died to save all who will accept Him. John 6:37 "…him that cometh to Me I will in no wise cast out." But we want to use every day to reach others. Help us by your prayers and in the coming day we shall rejoice together when we meet in the Glory Land. Until then pray and share the blessing!

Epilogue

Man reaches upward,
but not necessarily for God.
Man builds for the present,
but not always for eternity.
Man yearns for wealth
but not riches that will last.
He seeks power
but often ignores the One who has infinite power.

The Scripture says: *"Seek ye the Lord while He may be found, call ye upon Him while He is near."* Isaiah 55:6
"Whosoever shall call upon the name of the Lord shall be saved." Romans 10:13
"It is time to seek the Lord" Hosea 10:12

It Is Time To Seek The Lord

"It is time to seek the Lord.
Man reaches upward,
but not necessarily for God.
Man builds for the present,
but not always for eternity.
Man yearns for wealth
but not for riches that will last.
He seeks power
but often ignores The One who has infinite power. "
The Scriptures say, *"Seek ye the Lord while He may be found, call ye upon Him while He is near"* (Isa. 55:6). *"Whosoever shall call upon the name of the Lord shall be saved"* (Rom. 10:13). *"It is time to seek the Lord"* (Hos. 10:12).

May God Give Us Vision

"Where there is no vision, the people perish." Proverbs 29:18 Wallace and Ruth felt that the meaning of this verse was eminently clear so they asked God to give them a vision for the lost.

God answered their prayer.

They followed the pattern outlined in Scripture where the disciples of Christ were instructed to reach out further and further from their homes with the Gospel. *"You shall receive power when the Holy Spirit has come upon you; and you shall be witnesses to Me in Jerusalem, and in all Judea and Samaria, and to the end of the earth,"* (Acts 1:8 NKJV). Wallace Logan and his fiancee Ruth Sacher were both Christians with vision... first for their own families (their "Jerusalem"), whom the Lord graciously won to Himself.

Co-workers and friends (people in their "Judea") were witnessed to about the salvation they found in Christ.

Then to others beyond (their "Samaria"). They, along with others of their youth group, committed themselves to give a gospel tract to each home in the entire city of Buffalo, New York. The Lord enabled them to accomplish this goal, and He blessed their efforts.

God gave Wallace and Ruth a vision for people in distant lands, indeed, the opposite side of the world.

Having spent their lives profitably in service for the Lord Jesus Christ, they are now enjoying His presence in heaven. How eternally wise to have been involved in giving the Gospel to many and to have seen many come to Christ.

"Only one life, 'twill soon be past.

Only what's done for Christ will last."

For me to live is Christ.

May God give us this same vision to employ our time and to discipline our lives to live with eternity's values in view. Whatever time we have left to serve the King of Kings, let us dedicate it to the Master. "Oh God, give us vision for the lost, for the perishing. Oh Christ, give us the vision to reach those for whom You died."

African with no hands (No Hands To Thank God).

Frances and Esther Logan, twin nurses hold two sets of twins born at Chavuma Mission Hospital (see Some Tribal Customs).

Building with sun-dried bricks, each one measuring approximately 6×9×18 in. Wallace Logan is on right (see Early African Life).

Terry Fisher (l) and Bob Young (r) carrying marauding hyena that had been killed by villagers. Hyenas have been found to be not only scavengers, but in fact, predators (see Night Marauder).

1

Missionary children next to crocodile which, when alive, could take an adult human in seconds.

Talk about balance! This woman walks with ease carrying an impressive load on her head, in her left arm, and probably a baby on her back as well. In order to carry the significant load on her head, she not only displays excellent balance, but also an ergonomically sound gait by reducing to a minimum the up-and-down movement of the load on her head with each step and thus cuts down the amount of energy used. The result is a very graceful and efficient way to carry her load many miles.

Picture inside of the Tabernacle which could seat 2,000 people. The strong support poles—rivaling the strength and hardness of iron—seen along the left and right are the innermost core of tall iron-wood trees, shaved by hand with a sharp adz. The acoustics in the well-designed Tabernacle made it possible for the speaker to speak in normal volume and still be heard by all those in the building.

Mrs. Dorothy Barnett and her four children are pictured. In 1933, while on a Gospel safari with Wallace, her husband Fred died in a drowning accident on the Zambezi River. At the time of his death, the twin girls seen here were eight months old.

Handmade African marimbas with wooden keys are struck with wooden mallets, giving a mellow, attractive sound. Hollowed-out gourds of varying length can be seen beneath the keys to give better resonance.

A two-ox powered cart was a common mode of travel, especially for women and children (see Early African Life).

3

The sound of a wooden African drum suspended from a pole carried by two men, is a very effective mobile means to gather a crowd.

"Africa is a man's paradise." A typical couple traveling by foot shows one reason why. The man carries the status symbol, his walking stick; the woman carries everything else needed for the trip.

This 1912 photo was taken of Ruth Sacher-Logan's parents and siblings. At age sixteen, Ruth is in the back row, second from the right.

Traveling in an open pickup truck does make for faster travel, but does little for comfort!

Full GMC on it's way to villages for Gospel meetings.

'Likishi' (spirit man) dressed up as spirit, instills fear in people.

Traditionally, plates are nailed above the grave of the deceased husband for his use where he has gone. There is no compassion for the widow who is left with perhaps the entire stock of her kitchen (two plates) ruined and with nothing left for her use.

5

A dugout canoe crosses the Zambezi River with several seated passengers. Africans routinely stand as they paddle, demonstrating their excellent balance.

Wallace Logan, with a fellow evangelist on the back of his AJS motorcycle, leaves the mission station to preach the Gospel of Christ in outlying villages.

After the Sunday services, those who attended gather outside for a picture. This building was built as a meeting place for the Christians to gather. They make it available to be used as the local school as well.

Outside view of the Tabernacle which was designed by Wallace and built using unskilled, but willing workers.

Outdoor Breaking of Bread in 1932 (Early African Life).

The walls in this Gospel Hall in-the-making are built using sun-dried bricks. Seen in the foreground, these large bricks are made from clay-like mud using a locally made wooden mold. After drying in the sun, the bricks are ready for use. They are not, however, fired in a kiln.

The finished product has a thatched roof. Such a roof has a distinct advantage of being cool.

Wallace telling the Gospel story to those who may well have never heard it before. The standard pith helmet gave a small amount of cool comfort. It was also felt that it would prevent 'sunstroke.' It undoubtedly helped to lessen the likelihood of heat stroke.

First Gospel Hall – holds 100 (Early African Life).

Placement of grass thatched roof on Gospel Hall which is able to seat 500 (Early Life).

Inside view of Gospel Hall built for seating 500 (Early Life).

Heavily loaded wagon being drawn by many oxen.

An assembly of God's people outside a Gospel Hall. This is another example of shared use with the local school.

E.H. Sims liked donkeys for burden bearers on Gospel treks. Unfortunately lions liked them too—for dinner!

Arriving back at Chavuma by barge – welcome back crowd gathered (Barge trips).

Crossing on a bridge made of poles tied together with a child being carried (Early African Life).

Building a bridge for vehicles to cross.

A barge in very shallow water needs man (woman and child) power to be pushed to deeper water (Barge Trip).

These porters are carrying loads across a river on a Gospel safari (Early African Life).

Wallace, 9 years old with sister Jenny and brother David. Circa 1905.

These canoes are very heavy, having been fashioned from the trunk of a hardwood tree. The inside was dug out with a hand held adz (General Interest).

A witchdoctor accused this man of having an evil spirit. His punishment was to be held over a fire and fatally burned. God is gracious and in more than one case, both the witchdoctor and the surviving victim trusted Christ (White Man, Can You Help Me? in *A Man Called Sakuunda*).

Pontoons like this were used to cross vehicles over crocodile infested rivers (General Interest).

Here the Gospel Bus is being ferried by a pontoon across the deep Ko-bompo River in Zambia (Gospel Bus).

The sight of a large bus on a relatively small pontoon gave the (correct) impression that the whole thing was rather top heavy. Indeed, when the bus was driven onto the pontoon, thankfully stopping right at the correct place, the pontoon rocked forward and backward for a few heart-stopping moments. Prayer regularly preceded each pontoon experience.

With the bus on a bridge, travelers are filling the water tank of the bus with water from the river below.

Wallace ready for trekking on a Gospel Itinerary (Early African Life).

Someone has died in the village. Typically, the corpse was wrapped in a straw mat which served as the coffin. Years ago, sometimes instead of burial, the corpse was left where carnivorous animals could get to it (General Interest).

14

With the waters of the flooded Makondo River flowing over the bridge, people are walking on it to check for missing planks or other damage which would put the Gospel Bus at risk, say nothing about the driver.

People gathering on the periphery of the crowd to hear the Gospel presented through films projected on the screen atop the Gospel Bus (Gospel Bus).

The road across a plain flooded with six inches of water presents an interesting "highway" for the Gospel Bus to travel (Gospel Bus).

Village scene
with Ruth
pounding
cassava in
their mortar.

The baby twins were carried
in this kind of container when
itinerating with the Gospel.

Fetish with skull on pole – a form
of heathen worship (Early African
Life).